1

# 3-BOOK SERIES
## "QUANTUM CRISIS"

**Best Selling Author of**
**Quantum Crisis-II and Quantum Crisis-III**

**RAJ D. RAJPAL**
B.Sc.(Honors), D.A.P.R., D.M., D.C.S., D.M., M.B.A. (Ohio)

### QUANTUM CRISIS-I

Financial crises here afflicted Mankind from times immemorial. This publication is the first of a three-book commentary on the financial and credit problems facing the world today. In order to better understand this entire problem, it is critical to start from the origin of such world financial crises.

This book looks in detail at the most infamous and difficult financial crises in the past four hundred years. In this journey, the story weaves through diverse countries from Japan in the East to Scandinavia and the United Kingdom in Europe to the United States.

It has been found that a very common pattern exists in world financial crises, both past and present. Human greed and fear are the two essential components of all financial crises. Human greed accompanied with massive market speculation resulted in a run up in asset prices, creating an "asset bubble". This run up was then followed by a period of aggressive and uncontrolled selling of assets leading to a market meltdown. In the process, several investors and ordinary citizens got burnt— the winners at the other end of the table were the very privileged investors, who due to special insider information or connections with royalty and wealth got away with fraudulently earning an unprecedented amount of money.

The lessons to be learnt from this book are three-fold. Firstly, there is a dire need for more transparent investor education. Secondly, there is an immediate and urgent need for financial authorities to both develop comprehensive market regulation and to monitor risk management systems. Thirdly, there must be serious consideration of a way of Financial Life, which leads to a fundamental re-evaluation of human relationships. It is possible to be rich, yet honest and the book is dedicated to promoting the achievement of uncommon success in common circumstance.

ISBN : 978-0-9783550-3-6

**QUANTUM CRISIS-I**
Raighad
Global Financial Crises
RAJ D. RAJPAL

# QUANTUM CRISIS-I
## ORIGIN OF GLOBAL FINANCIAL CRISES

**Best Selling Author of**
**Quantum Crisis-II and Quantum Crisis-III**

---

**Best Selling Author of**
**Quantum Crisis-I and Quantum Crisis-III**

**RAJ D. RAJPAL**
B.Sc.(Honors), D.A.P.R., D.M., D.C.S., D.M., M.B.A. (Ohio)

### QUANTUM CRISIS-II

The global financial and credit crisis of 2007-2009 is like no other in the history of Mankind. This crisis has been sudden and unprecedented in the scale of its appearance and impact on humans all across this planet. It has fundamentally changed the nature of all financial relationships. A crisis of this magnitude and impact calls for a special and wide understanding of its causes, results and future implications. Development of this understanding constitutes the primary objective of this publication.

Slowly but surely the US real estate/mortgage crisis escalated into a US banking crisis, which then metamorphosed into a more dangerous international banking and credit crisis. The crisis spread its wings universally. This worldwide financial impact reinforces the fact that the world financial network is truly interconnected in every way. When America sneezes, Europe catches a cold while Asia inherits a transmitted flu.

The main culprits behind this crisis were the large investment and commercial banks in the US, who spread the across the world through sale of specialized, synthetic financial products. Using a process called "financial securitization" — risks of different qualities got wrapped up and sold as investment products globally. When Americans started defaulting on their mortgages, these toxic investment assets lost value and brought the entire money, credit and banking system to its knees.

This book attempts to navigate through some very complex financial territory and provides a 360 degree view of the crisis — attempting to propose some novel and radical ways of solving the problems tolerant to this crisis. This book is a must read for all individuals wanting an honest and unbiased view of the global financial and credit crisis.

The author prays that the new found understanding acquired through this book results in the reader saving, protecting and growing his nest egg more vigorously.

ISBN : 978-0-9783550-4-3

**QUANTUM CRISIS-II**
The Great Financial &
Credit Crisis
2007 - 2009
RAJ D. RAJPAL

# QUANTUM CRISIS-II
## THE GREAT FINANCIAL & CREDIT CRISIS
### 2007 - 2009

**Best Selling Author of**
**Quantum Crisis-I and Quantum Crisis-III**

---

**Best Selling Author of**
**Quantum Crisis-I and Quantum Crisis-II**

**RAJ D. RAJPAL**
B.Sc.(Honors), D.A.P.R., D.M., D.C.S., D.M., M.B.A. (Ohio)

### QUANTUM CRISIS-III

This book represents the final installment of the "Quantum Crisis" 3-book series. While "Quantum Crisis-I" dealt with the origin of financial crises, "Quantum Crisis-II" expounded the 2007-2009 global financial credit crisis. This book is a natural progression and attempts to provide solid time-tested savings, investment and risk management strategies to assist an investor accumulate his wealth better in a post crisis world.

In terms of financial planning processes, several good ideas are propounded in terms of retirement strategies, college education funding options, home investment and credit card reduction strategies. In addition, investment and insurance strategies as well as small business wealth creation processes are discussed. The purpose of all these separate and diverse strategies is to integrate the reader's financial portfolio with a view to it performing effectively and efficiently.

Since life is one big "ball of wax" comprised of a multitude of activities and relationships, the author urges the reader to step aside from his daily routine and look at the wider value of his Financial Existence. Personal health and wellbeing strategies, personal development processes and good mental, emotional and spiritual balance are all stressed as important components of a good overall Financial Life. Is there any value to money if you are unhappy and imbalanced in the process?

The author prays that an understanding and application of the numerous financial strategies help the reader better control costs, avoid future financial losses while aiding in the orderly and systematic growth of his hard-earned wealth.

ISBN : 978-0-9783550-5-0

**QUANTUM CRISIS-III**
Investment Strategies
For a New Global Reality
RAJ D. RAJPAL

# QUANTUM CRISIS-III
## WINNING INVESTMENT STRATEGIES TO PROSPER THROUGH THE GLOBAL FINANCIAL AND CREDIT CRISIS

**Best Selling Author of**
**Quantum Crisis-I and Quantum Crisis-II**

---

*AUTHOR SUGGESTS YOU READ ALL THREE BOOKS*
*SEQUENTIALLY FOR FULL UNDERSTANDING OF*
*GLOBAL FINANCIAL & CREDIT CRISIS*

2

# QUANTUM CRISIS I
## -ORIGIN OF GLOBAL FINANCIAL CRISES

By

# RAJ D.RAJPAL

B.Sc. (Honors), G.C.E. (Cambridge), D.A.P.R., D.M., D.C.S., D.P.S., M.B.A (Ohio)

**BEST-SELLING AUTHOR OF:**
**QUANTUM CRISIS 2: THE GREAT FINANCIAL & CREDIT CRISIS**
**2007-2009**
**&**
**QUANTUM CRISIS 3:**
**WINNING INVESTMENT STRATEGIES TO PROSPER THROUGH THE GLOBAL**
**FINANCIAL AND CREDIT CRISIS**
More info at: www.pioneer-communication.com

# PIONEER COMMUNICATION PUBLISHERS

## <u>BOOKS BOUTIQUE</u>

### *FINANCE SERIES*
**QUANTUM CRISIS 1**: THE ORIGIN OF FINANCIAL CRISES
**QUANTUM CRISIS 2**: THE GREAT FINANCIAL & CREDIT CRISIS
**QUANTUM CRISIS 3**: WINNING INVESTMENT STRATEGIES
TO PROSPER THROUGH THE FINANCIAL & CREDIT CRISIS
OFFSHORE INVESTMENTS: THE MILLIONAIRE VISION
OFFSHORE HAVENS: THE FOUR BEST-KEPT SECRETS OF
MILLIONAIRES

### *SALES AND MARKETING SERIES*
QUANTUM SELLING
QUANTUM SALES MANAGEMENT
QUANTUM MARKETING

### *MANAGEMENT SERIES*
QUANTUM ETHICS

### *SELF-IMPROVEMENT SERIES*
QUANTUM PUBLIC SPEAKING
YOU HAVE IT ALL NOW: YOUR LIFE IS TRULY YOURS TO
DISCOVER & ENJOY

### *OTHER FORTHCOMING BOOKS*
UNCONDITIONAL LOVE
UNCONDITIONAL YOGA
UNCONDITIONAL HEALTH
UNCONDITIONAL WEALTH
UNCONDITIONAL HEALING
UNCONDITIONAL SPIRITUALITY
UNCONDITIONAL WEIGHT LOSS

# QUANTUM CRISIS I

-ORIGIN OF GLOBAL FINANCIAL CRISES

By

# RAJ D.RAJPAL

B.Sc. (Honors), G.C.E. (Cambridge), D.A.P.R., D.M., D.C.S., D.P.S., M.B.A (Ohio)

National Quality Award Winner
Sales Coach and Public Speaker
Trainer, Bob Proctor Basic Program, Canada
Sales Trainer, Counselor Selling Program, U.S.A.
Trophy Winner, Public Speaking, Indo-American Society.
Provisional Applicant, Million Dollar Round Table, U.S.A.
Diploma, Graduate Advertising & Public Relations Program.
Uni-Lever Gold Medal Recipient-Graduate Marketing Management
Trainer, Bob Proctor Advanced Motivation Series Program, Canada.

**PIONEER COMMUNICATION**
www.pioneer-communication.com

PUBLISHER:
PIONEER COMMUNICATION, CANADA

Orders for additional books can be placed directly at:
www.pioneer-communication.com/rdrajpal@yahoo.com
National Library of Canada
Rajpal Raj D., 1951–
Quantum Crisis/Raj D. Rajpal
Includes Index
ISBN: 978-0-9783550-3-6

*This book is dedicated to the understanding of the serious challenges facing us--- as we set out to conquer this great global financial and credit crisis.*

*Awareness, understanding and meaningful investor actions are required in addition to total integration of personal, financial and spiritual priorities. This will help protect both one's inner peace and external wealth while guaranteeing a more sane and profitable future for our children.*

# TABLE OF CONTENTS

# PART ONE: THE BACKGROUND HISTORY OF PAST FINANCIAL CRISES

CHAPTER 6
THE DUTCH TULIP BUBBLE OF 1636

CHAPTER 7
THE SOUTH SEA BUBBLE OF 1720

CHAPTER 8
ADAM SMITH AND HIS IMPACT ON
THE US FINANCIAL SYSTEM

CHAPTER 9
ADAM SMITH RE-VISITED

CHAPTER 10
HAMILTON AND THE US FINANCIAL REVOLUTION
(1789-1795)

CHAPTER 11
AMERICA'S FIRST FINANCIAL CRISIS: THE PANIC OF 1819

CHAPTER 12
THE US FINANCIAL PANIC OF 1837

CHAPTER 13
SUMMARY OF MAJOR AND MINOR FINANCIAL PANICS
IN 19th CENTURY US

# PREFACE

2007 was a particularly challenging year for most investors. What started as a faint Headwind developed into a massive hurricane of unbelievable strength. The speed and impact of this financial hurricane was unprecedented in modern history.

October 2007 marked the beginnings of this financial hurricane. The impact of this unbelievably vital and destructive headwind was felt all over the world. The first manifestation of this devastation was felt intimately in the country, which represented the epicenter of this crisis---- the United States of America. The US stock market price values reflected the early symptoms of this larger financial malaise. In October 2007 it swung up and down ---- but the general trend was downwards. Stock prices depreciated expeditiously-----and this deep downward price decline spread to bond and commodity contracts too. Commodities, which were always thought to be a great hedge against future inflation, also saw precipitous drops in value. Nothing seemed safe anymore. All markets simultaneously tanked----- it was an unbelievable sell off. And, to add misery to madness, the Federal Reserve continued its path to lower interest rates, simultaneously decimating investors' interest savings and retirement returns for the older segment of the population.

All of a sudden nothing was safe anymore. All the financial advisors and their advice were not worth a dime.

In the backdrop of this vast destruction of investor and public wealth, was a notion in my mind that this was a subject worth investigating. I visualized myself being in a position to practically and positively assist a common investor in understanding and resolving these current and future financial risks. Looking at my over two decades of experience in risk management, I took upon myself the challenge to write a book which would, for the first time explain to the public the history, causes and effects of this financial tsunami. But to be valuable book, I would then have a continuing obligation and responsibility to present valid risk management initiatives to the personal investor with an end view of developing strategies to protect such investor's nest egg----- irrespective of whether this nest egg was a modest sum of money in a bank account or a multimillion dollar estate.

With these thoughts and feelings, I started this project of writing this monumental thesis. This book is more than sixty chapters long (counting present and future editions to this book).

The author humbly submits that an understanding of the causes and effects and practical action steps by an investor to mitigate such astronomic risks will go a long way to protect and enhance your life savings and life values.

May this book assist you in accomplishing such objectives.

# INTRODUCTION

This book's history starts in the United States. Where it ends is anyone's guess. But to be absolutely candid and forthright, the entire blame for this crisis rests in the hands of the most powerful country in the world--- the United States of America. Since this country marks the very epicenter of this financial earthquake, it is important to start the story in Part 2 with the goings on financially in this part of the Western World. This book therefore focuses greatly on this epicenter. How quickly we resolve this global financial and credit problem will rest on how well the financial repair is conducted in the United States.

The great financial and credit crisis of 2007-2009 amplified itself when greedy banks, insurance companies and other financial intermediaries/institutions (within the massive financial system) decided to systematically exploit the opportunities available to them. This was done with a view to maximize their profits with no consideration of what impact such profits would have on the global financial system.

At this time of our financial histories in the US, interest rates were very low----- this encouraged risk-taking by ordinary investors and speculators alike. With a negative real rate of borrowing, financial institutions lent billions of dollars out. This money landed up in everyone's hands. Such money was being invested in the ever-expanding real estate market as investors purchased homes and commercial properties with little or no money down (with very few credit restrictions).

This upward demand for real estate resulted in real estate prices hitting the roof nationally. Along with this investment behavior was the accompanying actions of investors to speculate in the stock and commodity markets. This resulted in ever increasing prices of everything from homes to office buildings to stock prices. The unlimited amount of capital available in the marketplace was largely due to a financial innovation called SECURITIZATION. Securitization was the magic financial engineering concept and technique, which assisted such financial institutions in creating and transporting these massive amounts of risk to third parties. By employment of the securitization process, banks, as one example, transferred their credit risks of lending money to third parties. In this process, banks were ably assisted by their evil counterparts in the investment banking system. The investment banks packaged and repackaged such bank loans into securities and sold them to different banks and investors all over the world. This is how an American problem became an international financial problem with "toxic assets" infecting all countries in the world and decimating global bank balance sheets. Let us try to understand the securitization process a bit better since this can be traced to the real roots of this financial and credit crisis. Securitization is a process where ordinary banks would resell their loans to investment banks, which then packaged them into loans of different tranches/qualities. Tranche 1, for example, could be loans made to individuals with good credit.

Tranche 2 were loans to individuals with average credit while Tranche 3 were loans made to questionable credit risks, like sub-prime borrowers.

Using this financial process banks were able to offload their loans to third parties. The third party would make an investment based on its risk-return requirement. If it wanted to earn a higher return it would invest in Tranche 2 as compared to Tranche 1.

As loan growth exploded in the US, more and more people were being allowed to borrow money to buy houses, which they could never afford (to pay back) by fraudulent banks and mortgage brokers. But this process of upward moving house prices could not go on forever. When the subprime borrowers started defaulting on their loan obligations, this started the process of collapse of the credit markets. There was so much money floating around and no investor really knew what any lenders portfolio was worth. This created confusion and finally panic in the marketplace. Where was one to invest? How would one know if one would get their money back after investing in say, a bank or other financial institution? Frankly, no one knew, because the toxic assets were neatly distributed in different parts of the financial system. Also no financial institution was willing to come clean on their real exposure to toxic assets. We got into an environment where everything was suspect. This resulted in the extreme stand by banks, which stopped trusting each other. Even for one bank to lend to another overnight became a problem. This started the credit crisis.

Since banks stopped or restricted lending, businesses could not get loans to continue their activities--- this resulted in them laying off workers, who now stopped spending money since they had less of it. The crisis had run a full circle. Easy lending, lots of money around, speculation and growth of asset markets followed with distrust, lack of confidence and a credit crisis. This resulted in job layoffs, lower consumer spending and a general lack of investor confidence. And the bottom line was that this crisis was impacting what hurts most, which is an average individual's ability to earn (as a result of a lost job) and his accompanying inability to spend. When you looked at the effect of this crisis on a macro-level, it invariably lead to economic disruption and downturn accompanied with a higher national unemployment rate, lack of consumer confidence and lower production of Gross National Product.

Many factors lead to this crisis. Inefficient and ineffective bank supervision, too lax an interest rate policy by the Federal Reserve and the massive securitization of loans by investment banks and regular banks all hand a hand in this crisis.

This book will slowly but surely take you through all the historical and actual steps in this evolving crisis. In the process, it will give you a bird's eye view of the problem and a 360-degree understanding of the crisis. It will then move forward to discuss policy prescriptions and most importantly look at what you can as a private investor do to protect and grow your nest egg.

This introduction serves to preview what is going to follow in his book. Read on--- the book is interesting and lively. May this presentation assist you in living a better financial and personal life and protect your hard earned assets.

# CHAPTER 1

## MISSION STATEMENT

The purpose of this book is unique in the sense that it tries to understand the whole picture reflecting the universal financial and credit crisis. This particular crisis is like no other since the Great Depression and therefore needs patient and clear understanding. The problems surrounding this crisis are very complex---- causes of this crisis which appear like simple concepts presented by the media and other vested interests do not reflect the fundamental reasons triggering this problem. There are numerous causes, some which appear on the surface and others more subliminal. In fact, it is the dangerous combination of a variety of lethal causes all acting at the same time, which has precipitated this crisis.

The book revolves around three different time curtains representing the past (Part 1), the present (Part 2 and Part 3) and the future (Part 3 and Part 4). The first part talks about what money represents and how and where it derives its power and influence from. This part continues as a historical journey into how money was created and what shape and form it appears in the present. The second part goes into the past history of bubbles, depressions and public mania. This history is critical in understanding what has happened in the past and how the string of past, present and future events are interlinked.

In this process, the reader understands that "financial crises" existed through many past centuries in almost every country in the world. Causes of the prominent crises are then elucidated with a moral or policy prescription at the end of each historical crises point. It is surprising that wise economists, financial institutions and representative governments have still not learnt to spot these irrational exuberances in advance----- nor have they learnt to set up effective risk management and risk mitigation systems to control such negative wealth destruction occurrences.

Part 3 explains what went wrong with the current global financial and credit crisis and what we can do to solve this problem immediately with the least amount of pain.

Part 4 then goes to the most important part of this publication---- which is, what you, as an ordinary investor can do to protect and build your nest egg. It is not enough to know and understand this crisis. What is critical at this stage is to apply this newfound knowledge to grow your wealth and guarantee your lifestyle for generations to come.

In short the mission statement is part history, part an understanding of current problems with the second half discussing causes and policy prescriptions to solve this problem in addition to preventing such financial catastrophes in the future. And the last part talks about the most important person in the world--- which is, of course YOU with all the financial challenges you must now face as you struggle to protect and grow your wealth.

In closing, the mission statement is to educate, enlighten and grow your understanding of the financial world in a straight, plain and factual manner. May this mission statement serve to protect you in every shape and form conceivable.

# CHAPTER 2

## PHILOSOPHY BEHIND A CRISIS

Times have indeed changed today. The global crisis in front of us has fundamentally changed the nature of our relationships with each other. In times of plenty and prosperity when no thought was given to money, people lived in nice homes and had secure jobs. The family looked forward to two vacations, one in the summer and one around Christmas. When money was not immediately available there was the reliable credit card, which could stave off any scarcities. While all of this was happening, inflation was generally controllable and there was always enough to spend in spite of the daily increases in the cost of living. And our marvelous home, the ultimate bastion of free enterprise would quietly go up in value every year. Everything was fine and dandy. This was until the global financial crisis hit home. And hit home it did and the effect was a very severe jolt into reality.

The first manifestations of the crisis were the plunging values of homes in most neighborhoods. In early 2005 the deceleration had started in the United States--- first with slight drops till suddenly home prices started decreasing exponentially. The final housing shock arrived sometime in 2008 when the mortgage on the home was greater than its market value ------this provided a homeowner with his first glimpse with scarcity and poverty. Still things were going along fine till the stock market tanked in 2008.

And October 2008 was like no other month or year. At around this time the US Government refused to bailout the investment banking firm, Bear Stearns, and everything went downhill subsequent to that. 2009 was a time of increased change as national consumer confidence plummeted and the US started losing jobs in the first two months of the year at a rate in excess of 500,000 jobs per month. Now, you had zero or inappreciable equity in your home, your stock market portfolio had tanked by over 50% and you either had or were in danger of losing your job. Suddenly there was a real crisis---- it was a personal crisis of unbelievable portions and the only story out there was one of personal survival.

This crisis changed in many ways the relationship between people. Everyone was so self-consumed in his or her financial and life issues that there was very little time for retrospection of the wider issues, which had created this problem. One of such issues was the relationship between the people and the global financial system. Did the controllers/primary players In the financial system have the right to decimate individual wealth? And how much greed (on their part) was enough? And now that the destruction was complete who would save us? America, which had always believed in the free enterprise system where the markets would sort out what is right and return to equilibrium suddenly realized that this business model, was ineffective and inefficient in solving the massive new financial problems.

Suddenly the Government had to sort out the mess to redistribute resources so that the problem could be solved and resources could be properly allocated among the different players in the financial system. And what about the financial architecture surrounding the financial system? Something was seriously wrong here too in a way where a few powerful constituents like global banks, investment banks, insurance companies and mortgage related entities proved that in the name of greed they had the power to destroy the otherwise worthwhile financial architecture?

The philosophy behind this crisis starts with a self-examination on the part of all components of this global financial system to understand their individual roles and effects and to design proper systems to insure stability and prosperity to everyone. As the financial crisis developed, it showed how few powerful constituents could destroy the lifestyle of billions of people worldwide.

The philosophy behind the crisis needed to deal with human values---- the basic values of self-respect, concern about other individual's rights and a desire to work cooperatively and peacefully knowing there was enough for everyone. The current crisis brought to the fore several ethical issues that expressed them in the total callousness and indifference of some financial players to the detriment and ruin of hundreds of small and medium sized players. And this abuse of ethics involved primarily the large financial organizations like the commercial and super powerful investment banks along with their brethren in insurance and mortgage companies.

Such large corporations in the United States (predominantly) violated the rights of everyone else to survive and prosper and given the interrelatedness of the global financial system such unconscionable and criminal behavior resulted in people suffering all over the world. All of a sudden there were 20 million people out of work (in early 2009) in China due to reduced global demand for their products in addition to millions of people displaced in Asia, Europe and Australia people who due to no fault of their own had become indirect negative beneficiaries of the global financial scam perpetrated by a few super large financial institutions in the United States.

Looking at this massive and catastrophic effect on individual's lives---- this destruction and suffering point to a time which has now come for the world to become one. By this I mean, there is a great and extreme need for humans to work co-operatively and peacefully in every field of endeavor. Globalization has become the first step, which has brought people and cultures in intimate contact with each other---- this has all started with a need to serve the needs of international business. However this movement is only the beginning.

The philosophy of good business ethics is intimately connected with this need for companies and individuals to honestly talk with one another. What invariably gets in the way of clear, honest communication is the presence of diversity of language and cultural backgrounds of all such parties to such conversation.

Also one has to be cognizant of the motivating factors behind such conversations, whether such purpose is to do business together or to understand each other better, religiously, physically and/or spiritually.

When we look at the state of ethics in this world, one cannot hide the fact that there is at every level and corner of this world a sense of disarray and disrepair caused by ceaselessly selfish acts of both individuals and groups. Let me explain. In order for us to grow together we need to be aware and alert of each other's needs. Only when such understanding is crystal clear can we hope to proceed with the arduous and challenging task of optimally relating to each other. Unfortunately, what is actually happening in the world is the reverse of this ideal process of communication. The individual, corporation or nation first thinks of all it priorities and then works out a way of relating with the other individual, corporation or nation. Therefore, there is no proper communication or relationship. The more powerful nation or corporation gets the upper hand in such relationships. The world as we see it now is in a constant state of war between the strong and the weak. The strong represent the haves of this world; the weak represent the have-nots. The stronger, more financially capitalized and agile company tends to dominate world markets and creates disharmonious relationships with its customers and the world at large. Surely, when Green Peace and other world-minded individuals and organizations protest at G-7 meetings, these protests represent some cause and reason.

I am not a member of the Green Peace organization nor do I belong to any other activist groups. But I know one thing for sure and that is the fact that the time has come when big and small nations, big and small corporations and corporations and lawmakers sit down and do something to clean up the mess. And what is this mess? It is the mess of unbridled exploitation of energy and financial resources. It is the filthy and unconscionable act of throwing up greenhouse gases to make a profit at any cost. It is actions made by groups of executives to rip off the public by financial misrepresentations and distortions. This nonsense needs to stop right now.

Although what is happening now ethically is very negative we must realize that even this cloud has a silver lining. Maybe the Lord has wanted all this to happen to bring us all together in a spirit of compromise, adjustment and peace.

The philosophy behind a global crisis points to a deeper and honest understanding of all the problems being created today as a result of a lack of concern for others. This philosophy also calls for all parties responsible for such "pollution" to sit together and talk earnestly with a view to solving such problems immediately and instantaneously. Corporations must talk to their customers, nations must talk with other nations, and people must talk with other people to overcome cultural gaps. We must all try hard to communicate and act together to save the world. This is not a Utopian vision. It is the truth. The World is decaying and dying slowly but surely. But this is not the end of Life or Existence.

We need to step back and look at the problems we have created and come back with a humble positive mind to undo all the wrongs of the past. This is absolutely possible given the depth and breadth of human intelligence. We have had the power to advance technologically; to send a man to the moon; to create numerous and marvelous scientific advancements and even to prolong life itself. Why can the human mind not go one step forward and solve this bigger problem it has created through poor communications and deplorable personal and business ethics?

In the solution to this problem lies our philosophical and real advancement. And the message is simple. To live together in this marvelous and wonderful world, we must understand why we seek to dominate others, why we seek to use unethical actions as an excuse to get ahead in our lives and how we can come together and all win together by respecting everyone's right to live, whether it is a poor man living in a slum in India or an African afflicted with AIDS.

The burning need today is for the human to work together with his fellow human to bring about good in the world. Good ethics, good conduct and proper action always starts and ends with the human being. Are we really ready to make this great inner change? On the answer to this question lies the hope and salvation of Mankind.

Work together honestly, help others and co-operate harmoniously and the World will always be there to supply all our needs.

Keep fighting and building walls, misrepresent constantly, continue expressing unethical behavior and feed greenhouse gases to the atmosphere and our world will cease to exist, as we know it. The choice is yours.

It is the author's fervent prayer, that we can make decisive and positive change at the individual, corporate and national level to make this world a better place for our children and us.

May this book be a small opening to get us into the vast expanse of universal consciousness, where everything is possible.

# CHAPTER 3
# PSYCHOLOGY OF A CRISIS

The current global financial and credit crisis had its intimate roots in the manifestation of human greed. How else can you explain the massive fraud, misrepresentation and cruel exploitation of financial players in the worldwide system? This greed was amplified by the superiority and secrecy of prevailing knowledge. Let me explain. Firstly, we need to put the blame where it is due. The blame primarily rests in the hands of the large US commercial and investment banks, along with other influential mega players, like US hedge funds, the US insurance leadership under AIG Insurance  and US mortgage related outfits like mortgage brokers, mortgage originators, mortgage re-sellers, and etcetera.

These large players engaged in severe and unconscionable gambling on an unprecedented scale. Their investment behavior had all the hallmarks of engaging in activities with unlimited upside potential and no downside investment risk. The commercial banks that sold home loans to the investment bank for further sale had no risk. They took the loan off their balance sheet the moment they sold it to the investment banks. There was zero risk for them. In an environment of low interest rates and rising home prices and availability of capital they lent billions of dollars to sub-prime borrowers, and immediately resold these loans to investment banks after making a substantial profit.

The investment banks then repackaged the loans into different Tranches (credit tranches) and sold it to institutional investors, foreign governments, and foreign banks through the mechanism of direct sales. They also had no skin in the game and could engage in shifting billions of dollars of risk all over the world. The differentiating factor for these investment package sales and what made them easily saleable was the paucity of information. This paucity of information was created by the employment of advanced financial engineering techniques. The securitization process was so complicated and devious that no one, save the investment banks themselves, knew exactly what was inside these loans. In such absence of information the investment community surrendered their collective intelligence and judgment to the well known US rating agencies. They believed that these rating agencies had exercised due diligence in analyzing and assessing the risk worthiness of these tranches of sub-prime and other mortgage loans. But the rating agencies themselves failed to exercise financial prudence in evaluating the appropriate risk of these investment vehicles. Such rating agencies erroneously labeled most of these real estate loans, packaged collaterized loans and other asset-backed mortgages as AAA never anticipating in their mathematical valuation models that the real estate market would show such significant downward correction. Huge banks and institutions all over the world bought these securities trusting the declared risk ratings provided.

However and very mysteriously none of these sophisticated investors paid attention to the inherent conflict of interest between the rating agencies and issuers of debt (which was being evaluated by the agencies). The non-palatable fact was that the that the issuers of debt like investment banks paid these rating organizations for their services---- one wonders how and why most of these securities were labeled AAA.

The financial crisis became serious when investors had no way of determining where the toxic assets were and therefore could not professionally value any specific investment. Since the toxic assets were everywhere, there was an immediate loss of investor confidence causing a lack of trust and confidence in the market. This led to the credit crisis and the deplorable market condition today.

Another important psychological factor, which involved the manipulation of other financial investors by these large banks and insurance companies basically, revolves around the issue of ethics. These large players exhibited very poor ethics in their business dealings with others as they decided to maximize profit at any cost with no regard to the values and needs of others.

Therefore, greed, a superiority based on having exclusive and protected knowledge about loans securitization (knowledge which the investment public did not have), and a poor sense of ethics all contributed to this financial mess the world is in now.

Let us now turn our attention to the issues surrounding the need for proper ethical behavior on part of these large financial institutions.

To understand ethical behavior one needs to look closely at human psychology. Human psychology is a fascinating subject. How and why we act and the results there from can fill thousands and thousands of pages of psychological material. Looking at our psychology in terms of ethics, we must first step in and understand our motivation factors. Abraham Maslow, a psychologist I respect a great deal, came up with a hierarchy of human needs pyramid. He believed that every action we took had its roots in our quest to fulfill a dominant need or desire. However, we tended to focus on first fulfilling basic needs, like the need for food, water and shelter. After we achieved this, we moved on to our safety and physiological needs. Then we spent our energy in meeting with our self-esteem needs and so on........

What does an understanding of Maslow's hierarchy of needs have to do with the psychology of ethics? I believe it has a lot to do with a deeper understanding of this subject matter. Depending on which part of the world you live in and your current economic and political situation, you may be forced to behave in certain ways. If you live in India in a slum, your day-to-day life may involve struggling to get enough bread, water and salt for your family. With a lack of abundant jobs in your community accompanied by the ever-increasing financial demands from your family, you may be forced to lie, cheat and steal to survive.

On the other hand, if you live in the vast profitable expanse of North America, you may not have the same sense of economic urgencies as a poor Indian.

You probably are paying for a home and have a decent job and worthwhile material comforts. What causes you to lie and cheat and steal?

Coming back to Maslow's pyramid, you are probably attempting to fulfill your needs and desire to get rich quicker than at your usual normal pace. This invariably is what happened to the executives who went to jail when associated with Enron Corporation in the US. These executives were rich; they enjoyed positions of power and influence. However, that was not enough for them. In order to get richer faster they took shortcuts. However, these shortcuts created end results, which were devastating to the lives of thousands of employees at Enron Corporation. Many of these employees lost their entire jobs and life savings and retirement pensions.

So, if you live in a developed economy, you may decide to cheat, lie and steal to get up the corporate ladder faster or to make a fast buck period... There is no other motivating factor to be unethical here.

How do we change this human psychology of survival in India and other developing economies and the preponderance of greed in North America, Europe and most of the developed world??

This is a very difficult question to answer. And in the proper answer and implementation of such answer lies the solution to the ethical dilemmas all around this world.

In order to stem and control the ethical issues, a host of national and international regulations have sprung up.

The Sarbanes-Oxley Act in the US was passed into law soon after the Enron scandal. The United Nations has recommended model corporate governance standards after reviewing all the worldwide problems in the corporate ethics field.

Therefore, we have two sides of a coin, both of which can help solve the problem.

Educate the people; make them more aware of what they are doing wrong; present the social penalties for wrongful action [set up a strong judiciary and police system to monitor ethical performance and develop the societal laws to discourage ethical abuse. Bring the citizens into the picture by large page ads. Show them the cost of unethical behavior to their livelihood and to the nation and world at large. Ask them to become whistleblowers, if they notice or suspect unethical activity at any personal, private, business or corporate level. Give them a monetary reward for spotting and reporting on potentially criminal unethical activity. In India, the Income tax department gives a percentage of the department's recovery of unpaid taxes to the ordinary citizen, who spots and reports someone not paying his fair share of taxes. Why can we not make this a model policy on a worldwide scale? Get the common man to report on unethical behavior. Neither government nor the entire United Nations can effectively police this problem with bad ethics on a consistent basis without the aid of the common man.

The solution to the unethical dilemma philosophically is to pull all stops out and get everyone involved in solving the problems.

Successful solution of this problem at a personal, societal, and judicial/police level will result in better allocation of world resources and a more efficient and productive world. Each and every human being has a responsibility to make the world a better place to live in. This is the first step in solving this problem and removing this curse from this world.

In closing, the challenge in solving the global financial and credit crisis is to be able to understand the driving psychological factors behind this problem: unbelievable greed, an information superiority in terms of the development of exotic financial instruments like securitization and a blatant expression and abuse of personal and business ethics.

All these three psychological factors caused the major problem the world is in now.

# CHAPTER 4

## PSYCHOLOGY OF A CRISIS REVISITED

I feel at this juncture that it makes sense to understand what happened and caused this global crisis. A clear understanding of the problems (on a psychological level) should hopefully prevent this type of crisis from re-occurring in the future. As I had indicated in the last chapter the crisis was caused by massive greed, information manipulation and poor ethics by the large financial houses in the United States. On closer examination, greed, which is the predominant cause of this behavior, has a deep and interconnected relationship with ethics. Poor ethics represents itself in the manifestation of greed and therefore I have attached this chapter for perusal, study and discussion. All I am talking about in this chapter is definitions, understanding and expression of both personal and business ethics; it is my hope that this understanding will help governments and other responsible financial authorities in setting up checks and balances in the system to catch irresponsible, fraudulent and unethical behavior so that such a crisis can never reoccur in the future. It is with this understanding that I am paying particular attention to the subjects surrounding personal and business ethics. Let us now move forward to an understanding of both personal and business ethics.

Wikipedia Encyclopedia defines Ethics as, "Ethics is a major branch of philosophy, which encompasses right conduct and good life. It is significantly broader than the common conception of analyzing right and wrong. A central aspect of ethics is 'the good life,' the life worth living or life that is satisfying, which is held by many philosophers to be more important than moral conduct. The major problem is the discovery of the summun bonum, the greatest good."

Some of the core issues in the study of ethics are:

1. Justice
2. Value
3. Right
4. Duty
5. Virtue
6. Equality
7. Freedom
8. Trust
9. Free will
10. Consent
11. Moral responsibility

Now that the Wikipedia definition is established, let us move along with details on the described components of ethics.

## 1. JUSTICE

Personal ethics involves the application of justice. In your dealings with others, are you following the code of law established in your community?

Are you dealing fairly and justly with your neighbor and friend? In your business relationships involving your customers are you seeking to provide the best behavior in consonance with the legal codes?

## 2. VALUE

In terms of value, are you offering a product or service, which represents an ultimate storehouse of value? Is the price of the product commensurate with its quality and embedded service promises? In terms of personal relationships with family and friends, is your relationship one, which embodies the application of the highest standard of value?

## 3. RIGHT

Do your personal and business actions involve doing something, which is generally regarded as being right? Or are your actions in a gray area---- you are acting legally but have exhibited improper moral behavior. You understand that the law expects certain minimum standards of moral behavior, but that you may be in fact doing something legal and yet something immoral (not right).

4.  DUTY

In every situation and interaction with others, are you discharging your duty to the relationship fully and wholly, with no regard to the amount of time, attention or energy expended by you in this process?

5.  VIRTUE

The best way of expressing the application of virtue is by quoting from the Bible. The Holy Bible: New Revised Standard Version quotes in Galatians 5:22-23: virtue being:

"Love, joy, peace, patience, kindness, generosity, faithfulness, gentleness and self-control."

The central question the reader must ask himself is if he exercising the above virtues in his dealings with others.

6.  EQUALITY

In your everyday relationships, do you approach matters respecting other's right to live and think freely? In business matters, where you seek to influence others, are you approaching your customer with a fair and level sense of equality? Or are you trying to exploit the relationship because of your special and unique status, resources and power?

7.  FREEDOM

Are your actions conducted in an environment of personal freedom? And are you dealing with others while respecting their freedom to agree or disagree with your proposition?

Do you accept another's option to accept or reject your ideas and proposition, thereby exercising their personal freedom even if this means your idea or acceptance being put at risk?

8. FREE WILL

When interacting with others, are you conducting your affairs armed with complete self- knowledge of your actions and behaviors? Is your conduct a result of an exercise of free will unabated and uninfluenced by peer or pressure groups? Are you doing what you believe is the best possible thing for your loved one, friend or customer? In short, are you exercising free will all the time?

9. CONSENT

In your everyday actions, are you making sure that you take the consent of all affected parties in your relationships? Or are you taking their involvement in the relationship as granted?

10. MORAL RESPONSIBILITY

Are you aware of your moral responsibilities in communications with others? Are you taking the time to understand and study the impact of your behavior and business interactions with others? Are you enhancing someone else's life? Or are you merely ripping them off?

## RELATIONSHIPS BETWEEN ETHICS AND MORALS

Coming back to definitions from Wikipedia, the following further clarifications are provided in terms of the relationships between a study of ethics and morals. Further, there is a good definition of personal ethics. Here are the definitions:

"Ethics and morals are respectively akin to theory and practice. Ethics denotes the theory of right action and the greater good, while morals indicate their practice.

Personal ethics signifies a moral code applicable to individuals, while social ethics means moral theory applied to groups. Social ethics can be synonymous with social and political philosophy, in as much as it is the foundation of a good society or state. Ethics is not limited to specific acts and defined moral codes, but encompasses the whole of moral ideals and behaviors, a person's philosophy of life."

ETHICS AND THE WISE GREEK PHILOSOPHERS

Several Greek philosophers, countless centuries back, had a basic awareness of what ethical action was. According to Socrates, knowledge, which had an intimate connection with human life, was the most important type of knowledge.

Socrates propounded the system of " self-knowledge" as the most important knowledge center. Awareness was the key to good self-knowledge. If a person was aware of the impact of his actions on him and the society at large and had the capacity and capability of distinguishing right from wrong, society would comprise of more wiser citizens and less crime would be committed. Happiness and harmony would result as a direct effect of such enlightened awareness and action.

Another great Greek philosopher, Aristotle envisaged a system of ethics under the heading of the term," self-realizationism." What he meant by this term was that all individuals were born with certain specific and unique talents.

If individuals acted according to their built in nature and used their God-given talents, they would be more content and complete. As a result man should live with moderate virtue. This is normally difficult since this implies doing the right thing, to the right person, at the right time, to the proper extent, in the correct fashion, for the right reason.

To close this chapter, an intimate awareness and knowledge of personal ethics is a starting point and foundation for all human relationships. If one can understand and accept these values, then individuals can work together more fairly.

Business relationships will improve as a result and the incidence of exploitation will decrease. Also, if individuals approach their personal lives with such high standards, then ultimately this will result in better family and community relationships. Everything starts and ends with the individual.

To create a lasting and permanent change in the world ethically, the Individual will need to take the first steps in understanding and modifying his behavior for the greater social good. He will need to understand that he is linked with his family, community, business and world around him. Good actions at all levels will create stellar relationships at all levels of existence. This will make the community and world a better and more harmonious place to live in---- a world in which people learn to share and celebrate differences and not a world where talent, money and power control future results.

## BUSINESS ETHICS

Business Ethics may be defined as, "a form of the art of applied ethics that examines ethical principles and more or ethical problems that can arise in a business environment." Put simply, business ethics has to do with the ethical value of decisions made by businesses in their quest for profits.
Let us now look at the various issues corporations face as they react and interact with all the different people they do business with.

GENERAL ETHICAL CONSIDERATIONS
The following are some of the areas, which create perceptions of unethical or ethical behavior on part of the corporation:
AREA 1
FUNDAMENTAL OBJECTIVES OF BUSINESS
On a very fundamental basis, one needs to ask why the corporation exists in the first place. If we review the Anglo-American model, which is prevalent in the United Kingdom, the United States and Canada, we understand the predominant and primary reason for doing business from the corporation's perspective is to maximize value for their shareholders. If corporations engage and act on this narrow view at the detriment of relationships with all the other stakeholders, like suppliers, customers and competitors, to name a few, then this process of shareholder maximization at the expense of all other interested parties could be generally viewed as unethical behavior.

AREA 2
CONTRIBUTION TO CORPORATE SOCIAL RESPONSIBILITIES
Another way of assessing the quality of ethics in a corporation is to examine their corporate social responsibility mission. If the corporation talks about such responsibilities but never gets off ground zero to take an active interest and involvement in social causes, then this again can be viewed as unethical activity.

AREA 3
INTER-COMPANY RELATIONSHIPS
How companies behave with each other, particularly when they are in neck-to-neck competition defines their ethical role. When a company sees its competitor as getting weak and exercises an aggressive hostile takeover bid or when a corporation pays someone to spy on its competitors (industrial espionage) determines its outlook to business and ethics in general.

AREA 4
POLITICAL CONTRIBUTIONS AND LOBBYING EFFORTS
The extent of political contributions and the capital expended on lobbying for continuation of existing products and addition of new ones provides the ethical flavor of a company. For example, a tobacco company paying a lobbyist in Washington to get generous advertising exposures for cigarettes can be viewed as a highly unethical action.

## A) ACCOUNTING INFORMATION ETHICS

Here are some examples of unethical accounting information use.

### Creative accounting scams

The behavior of Enron Corporation in the US is a very good example of how hiding liabilities and misreporting income created a massive problem for everyone who was associated with this company. Briberies and kickbacks When corporations bribe government officials in order to seek government contracts, this constitutes anti-competitive behavior and results in misallocation of societal resources. Insider trading refers to an executive or other interested party having information in advance of public knowledge. For example, if a company is going to start selling a new product after receiving governmental approval, a fact which could increase its stock price. The manufacturing vice-president of this company has this information in advance and seeks purchase of his company shares in advance, knowing that once this announcement is made the share price will rocket upwards and he can make a quick profit. This definitely constitutes unethical behavior.

## B) HUMAN RESOURCE MANAGEMENT AND UNETHICAL BEHAVIOR

Human resources ethics deals with all relationships between an employer and an employee. In such relationships, the employer usually has an upper hand. When we view how the corporation is treating its employees, we then get an idea of the extent of ethical or unethical b behavior on part of the corporation. Here are some examples of corporate behavior in this field:

(i) Discrimination issues surrounding age, gender, race, religion, and disabilities among other factors.

(ii) Factors dealing with representation of employees like actions involving union busting, etcetera

(iii) Actions involving infringement of employee privacy without specific permission and authorization by concerned employee like video, Internet and telephone surveillance of employees and drug testing.

(iv) Occupational safety and employee health issues.

## C)    MARKETING AND SELLING ETHICS

Several issues abound on unethical use of marketing strategies, techniques and plans of action. These areas cover the following:

- (i)     Price fixing, price discrimination and price skimming
- (ii)    Unethical marketing strategies like the Ponzi scheme, Spam electronic marketing, pyramid schemes and planned obsolescence techniques.
- (iii)   Dangerous and unethical advertising content in the form of subliminal advertising and misrepresentation of product properties.
- (iv)    Unethical exploitation of children through specially designed advertisements.
- (v)     Unethical representation of products and services by salespeople representing a corporation.

## D    PRODUCTION ETHICS

The ethics of production has to do with the processes used to produce a product and how ethically a corporation engages in such processes. Here are some of the concerns in the production area:

- (i)     Defective, addictive and inherently dangerous products and services (like tobacco, alcohol, weapons manufacturing and bungee jumping).

(ii)    Production processes causing industrial waste into our rivers and general environmental pollution through greenhouse gases, etcetera.

(iii)   Problems arising out of new technologies like genetically modified food.

(iv)    The business of product testing ethics such as animal testing of products.

## E    INTELLECTUAL PROPERTY ETHICS

Intellectual property rights are intangible in nature. They are concerned with who has the rights to develop an idea.

Here are some areas of concern:

(1)   For example, if an author writes a new book and finds most or all his ideas plagiarized, then this constitutes an intellectual property right infringement.

(2)   Issues dealing with patent infringement.

(3)   Issues dealing with copyright and trademark infringement.

## SIGNIFICANCE OF BUSINESS ETHICS

Since most businesses in the world are in corporate form, how such businesses behave and interact becomes crucial. Here are some of the reasons for the importance of the study of business ethics:

1.   There is progressively greater power and influence exerted by corporations on the daily lives of people.

2. Big businesses have the potential power to positively assist or negatively destruct the communities they serve.
3. Businesses have the ability to effect the environment and their immediate communities positively or negatively.
4. With greater pressure being exerted by stakeholders like suppliers, other competitors, it becomes real important to understand how and when corporations should respond to such pressures and what constitutes acceptable behavior in this department.

## GLOBALIZATION & ITS IMPACT ON BUSINESS ETHICS

When corporations move away from their normal place of doing business into a new territory or country, several new issues come to the forefront. These are basically legal, accountability and cultural issues. Since the legal framework of doing business shifts when one moves from say, a developed nation to a developing economy, what rules of conduct are OK? The country of incorporation rules of the corporation? The rules of the emerging nation, where it seeks to do trade and investments? Who is going to police the business actions of the corporation now? What about cultural issues? How is the corporation to adapt to a totally different cultural expectation surrounding their products or services?

And what about accountability issues? Since the corporation does not really report on a daily basis to anyone, and since it does not have to be held accountable on numerous fronts, how does it serve its accountability responsibilities?

Several of these areas are gray areas. By this I mean, there is no definite standard of conduct here. And this is where most of the misunderstandings and mistrust lies for such multinational corporations.

The United Nations, with a view, to setting up some standards for international trade, business and conduct has suggested the achievement of 8 Millennium Development goals by 2015.

On the United Nations website, "www.undp.org", the following goals are listed:

Goal 1: Eradicate extreme poverty and hunger

Goal2: Achieve universal primary education

Goal 3: Promote gender equality and empower women

Goal 4: Reduce child mortality

Goal 5: Improve maternal health

Goal 6: Combat HIV/AIDS, malaria and other diseases

Goal 7: Ensure environmental sustainability

Goal 8: Develop a global partnership for development

Why am I talking about the United Nations goals? And what does this have to do with business ethics? Simply that since corporations are now becoming multinational in character and have the power to gain and profit from exposure to opportunities all over the world that this opportunity also entails a responsibility on their part.

If you are taking from the world then you must also give back to it. And what better way to give back than to assist the United Nations fulfills its eight major goals for the world. Therefore, if corporations are to be seen as truly caring and concerned global players, they must design and execute their strategies with a view to achieving one or more of these eight goals. Merely paying lip service or designing slick website content on their commitment to world issues is not enough. The message to them is: "Put your money where your mouth is. You simply cannot exploit the world masses. Now is the time to pay back for all your profits and success. Prove that you are really a caring corporate citizen".

This is why the corporation's role in helping the UN will go a long way in improving their credibility and enhancing their reputation as a caring, concerned world player.

## THE CASE FOR SUSTAINABILITY

Right through the world, time boundaries apart, more and more people are questioning the ethical behavior of corporations as they plunder and rape the natural resources of this world. Corporate ethical standards are now being applied to include the role of the corporation in respecting and nourishing the resources around it. Issues like pollution creation, the dumping of greenhouse gases, the issues surrounding product recyclability are all creating a framework, where a corporation will be forced to work environmentally and ecologically creatively to preserve the natural balance of the world.

The corporation will need to prove that it is indeed a corporate citizen of the world and cares not only for the goal of making profits but also in playing its part in keeping the balance in Earth between companies and their natural environments.

## THE TRIPLE BOTTOM LINE INITIATIVE

Triple bottom line is a phrase coined by John Elkington in 1994. It refers to the triple responsibility of a corporation to take care of the 3 P's: People, Planet and Profit. People in this equation refer to the social responsibilities of corporations.

Planet refers to the environmental responsibilities, including the cause of sustainability by companies. Profit represents what most corporations are in business for anyway.

Triple bottom line actions represent a new way of defining a corporation's responsibility. Instead of a corporation merely maximizing revenue for its shareholders, it now is called to contribute equally to a clean and sound ecological environment and to take positive steps to support all stakeholders. A stakeholder refers to anyone, who is effected directly or indirectly by the actions of the firm.

The stakeholder theory suggests that the firm should be used as vehicle for satisfying and coordinating stakeholder interests, instead of solely maximizing shareholders profit.

In real and practical terms these are some of the actions and initiatives to be taken by a firm to satisfy the triple bottom initiative of People, Planet and Profit.

In order to serve the People/Human Capital initiative a firm needs to have fair and beneficial practice towards labor and the community at large.

In order to ably serve the Planet/Natural capital initiative it needs to benefit the natural order as much as possible by conducting a life cycle assessment of all products manufactured.

This is done to calculate the actual and true environmental cost of growth and harvesting of raw materials to manufacture to distribution to eventual disposal by the end user.

All processes to optimize the ecological and environmental impact of production are taking into consideration by such company. In order to serve the profit initiative the corporation must make a real contribution financially and economically to all the markets it serves.

## CONCLUSION

The global financial crisis has shown the ruthless and exploitive of large financial institutions and their leaders. To a great extent, these corporations and their senior management stand guilty in violation of most personal and business ethics principles elucidated in this chapter.

From Bernard Madoff and his 50 billion dollar Ponzi scheme to defraud investors to a president of an investment bank who invested more than one million dollars on his office furniture, these examples represent the reasons why this global crisis is like no other. And to come out of this mess will require the coordinated and co-operative effort of all world nations and world people. It is simply too big a problem to be solved by any one country or any group of people. Understanding this massive violation of personal and business ethics should provide a guideline to everyone to measure their personal and business behavior according to a higher ethical standard. We are all in this mess and we all need to work together to develop a higher ethical consciousness---- this consciousness and understanding will work wonders to accelerate the solution of the problem.

# CHAPTER 5
# HISTORY OF MONEY

Before we can start to understand the nature of the financial crisis, we need to understand what money is, how it came about and what role it plays in an individual's life. Understanding its functions and utilities would then help us understand its role in the global financial system and hopefully assist the reader in understanding the entire problem surrounding this crisis.

Money means different things to different people. The value of money is influenced by where you live and what you are able to buy with a fixed quantum of it. In the United States the US dollar is the standard store of value. However, in India, say, the Indian rupee is the standard definition of money. To an Indian a US dollar means very little. The only impact it has is when the country buys imported products like oil or export products worldwide or when trade deficits have to be settled in foreign currencies. But for the ordinary Indian citizen what matters simply is how well he can live given the purchasing power of his resources.   But currency aside, money has no value unless it can create a power to buy something---- in that sense; it is a both a medium of exchange in addition to be a long-term storehouse of value. The history of money spans thousands of years.

Many items have been used as commodity money such as naturally scarce precious metals, conch shells, barley, beads etc., as well as many other things that are thought of as having value.

Modern money (and most ancient money) is essentially a token — in other words, an abstraction. Paper currency is perhaps the most common type of physical money today. However, objects of gold or silver present many of money's essential properties. The term price system refers to how societies, communities and nations determine the conversion value of a unit of their currency.

## The emergence of money

The Sumer civilization developed a large scale economy based on commodity money. The Babylonians and their neighboring city states later developed the earliest system of economics as we think of it today, in terms of rules on debt, legal contracts and law codes relating to business practices and private property.[1][2]

The **Code of Hammurabi** (*Codex Hammurabi*), the best preserved ancient law code, , was created ca. 1760 BC in ancient Babylon. It was enacted by the sixth Babylonian king, Hammurabi. Earlier collections of laws include the codex of Ur-Nammu, king of Ur (ca. 2050 BC), the Codex of Eshnunna (ca. 1930 BC) and the codex of-Ishtar of Isin (ca. 1870 BC).[3]These law codes formalized the role of money in civil society.

They set amounts of interest on debt... fines for 'wrong doing'... and compensation in money for various infractions of formalized law.

The Shekel referred to an ancient unit of weight and currency. The first usage of the term came from Mesopotamia circa 3000 BC. and referred to a specific mass of barley which related other values in a metric such as silver, bronze, copper etc. A barley/shekel was originally both a unit of currency and a unit of weight... just as the British Pound was originally a unit denominating a one pound mass of silver.

The use of proto-money may date back to at least 100,000 years ago. Trading in red ochre is attested in Swaziland. Shell jewelry in the form of strung beads also dates back to this period,[4] and had the basic attributes needed of early money, such as being scarce in inland areas, and not easily counterfeited. Also they were 'worked' to be made into something using a technique... or workmanship, into an attractive object, that may have been considered then, valuable.

In cultures where metal working was unknown, shell or ivory jewelry were the most divisible, easily storable and transportable, scarce, and hard to counterfeit objects that could be made. It is highly unlikely that there were formal markets in 100,000 BC (any more than there are in recently observed hunter-gatherer cultures).

Nevertheless, proto-money would have been useful in reducing the costs of less frequent transactions that were crucial to hunter-gatherer cultures, especially bride purchase, splitting property upon death, tribute, and inter-tribal trade in hunting ground rights ("starvation insurance") and implements.

In the absence of a medium of exchange, all of these transactions suffer from the basic problem of barter — they require an improbable coincidence of wants or events. Overcoming this without money requires some system of in-kind "credit" or "gift exchange", restricting trade to those who know one another.

## Commodity Money

Bartering has several problems, most notably the coincidence of wants problem, but even if a farmer growing fruit and a wheat-field farmer need what the other produces a direct barter swap is impossible for seasonal fruit that would spoil before the grain harvest. A solution is to indirectly trade fruit for wheat through a third, "intermediate", commodity: the fruit is exchanged for this when it ripens.

If this *intermediate commodity* doesn't perish and is reliably in demand throughout the year (e.g. copper, gold, or wine) then it can be exchanged for wheat after the harvest.

The function of the intermediate commodity as a store-of-value can be standardized into a widespread commodity money, reducing the coincidence of wants problem. By overcoming the limitations of simple barter, commodity money makes the market in all other commodities more liquid.

Where trade is common, barter systems usually lead quite rapidly to several key goods being imbued with monetary properties. In the early British colony of New South Wales, rum emerged quite soon after settlement as the most monetary of goods. When a nation is without a fiat currency it commonly adopts a foreign fiat currency. In some prisons where conventional money is prohibited, it is quite common for cigarettes to take on a monetary quality, and throughout history, gold has taken on this unofficial monetary function.

From early times, metals, where available, have usually been favored for use as proto-money over such commodities as cattle, cowry shells, or salt, because they are at once durable, portable, and easily divisible. The use of gold as proto-money has been traced back to the fourth millennium B.C. when the Egyptians used gold bars of a set weight as a medium of exchange, as the Sumerians had done somewhat earlier with silver bars.

The first stamped money (having the mark of some authority in the form of a picture or words) was introduced about 650 B.C. in Lydia.[5]

Coinage was widely adopted across Ionia and mainland Greece during the sixth century eventually leading to the Athenian Empire's 5th century B.C., dominance of the region through their export of silver coinage, mined in southern Attica at Laurium and Thorikos. A major silver vein discovery at Laurium in 483 BC led to the huge expansion of the Athenian military fleet. Competing coinage standards at the time were maintained by Mytilene and Phokaia using coins denominated in Electrum, Aegina in silver.

It was the discovery of the touchstone, which led the way for metal-based commodity money and coinage. Any soft metal can be tested for purity on a touchstone, allowing one to quickly calculate the total content of a particular metal in a lump. Gold is a soft metal, which is also hard to come by, dense, and storable.

As a result, monetary gold spread very quickly from Asia Minor, where it first gained wide usage, to the entire world. Using such a system still required several steps and mathematical calculation. The touchstone allows one to estimate the amount of gold in an alloy, which is then multiplied by the weight to find the amount of gold alone in a lump.

To make this process easier, the concept of standard coinage was introduced. Coins were pre-weighed and pre-alloyed, so as long as the manufacturer was aware of the origin of the coin, no use of the touchstone was required.

Coins were typically minted by governments in a carefully protected process, and then stamped with an emblem that guaranteed the weight and value of the metal. It was, however, extremely common for governments to assert the value of such money lay in its emblem and thus to subsequently debase the currency by lowering the content of valuable metal.

Although gold and silver were commonly used to mint coins, other metals could be used. For instance, Ancient Sparta minted coins from iron to discourage its citizens from engaging in foreign trade. In the early seventeenth century Sweden lacked more precious metal and so produced "plate money," which were large slabs of copper approximately 50 cm or more in length and width, appropriately stamped with indications of their value. Metal based coins had the advantage of carrying their value within the coins themselves — on the other hand, they induced manipulations: the clipping of coins in the attempt to get and recycle the precious metal. A greater problem was the simultaneous co-existence of gold, silver and copper coins in Europe. English and Spanish traders valued gold coins more than silver coins, as many of their neighbors did, with the effect that the English gold-based guinea coin began to rise against the English silver based crown in the 1670s and 1680s. Consequently, silver was ultimately pulled out of England for dubious amounts of gold coming into the country at a rate no other European nation would share.

The effect was worsened with Asian traders not sharing the European appreciation of gold altogether — gold left Asia and silver left Europe in quantities European observers like Isaac Newton, Master of the Royal Mint observed with unease.[6]

Stability came into the system with national Banks guaranteeing to change money into gold at a promised rate; it did, however, not come easily. The Bank of England risked a national financial catastrophe in the 1730's when customers demanded their money be changed into gold in a moment of crisis. Eventually London's merchants saved the bank and the nation with financial guarantees.

Another step in the evolution of money was the change from a coin being a unit of weight to being a unit of value.

A distinction could be made between its commodity value and its specie value. The difference in these values is seigniorage.[7]

The system of commodity money in many instances evolved into a system of representative money. This occurred because banks would issue a paper receipt to their depositors, indicating that the receipt was redeemable for whatever precious goods were being stored (usually gold or silver money). It didn't take long before the receipts were traded as money, because everyone knew they were "as good as gold".

Representative paper money made possible the practice of fractional reserve banking, in which bankers would print receipts above and beyond the amount of actual precious metal on deposit. So in this system, paper currency and non-precious coinage had very little intrinsic value, but achieved significant market value by being backed by a promise to redeem it for a given weight of precious metal, such as silver. This is the origin of the term "British Pound" for instance; it was a unit of money backed by a Tower pound of sterling silver, hence the currency is referred to as the Pound Sterling. For much of the nineteenth and twentieth centuries, many currencies were based on representative money through use of the gold standard. In the 600s there were local issues of paper currency in China and by 960 the Song Dynasty, short of copper for striking coins, issued the first generally circulating notes. A note is a promise to redeem later for some other object of value, usually specie. The issue of credit notes is often for a limited duration, and at some discount to the promised amount later.

## Fiat money

Fiat money refers to money that is not backed by reserves of another commodity. The money itself is given value by government fiat(Latin for "let it be done") or decree, enforcing legal tender laws, previously known as "forced tender", whereby debtors are legally relieved of the debt if they (offer to) pay it off in the government's money.

By law the refusal of "legal tender" money in favor of some other form of payment is illegal, and has at times in history (Rome under Diocletian, and post-revolutionary France during the collapse of the assignats) invoked the death penalty. Governments through history have often switched to forms of fiat money in times of need such as war, sometimes by suspending the service they provided of exchanging their money for gold, and other times by simply printing the money that they needed. When governments produce money more rapidly than economic growth, the money supply overtakes economic value. Therefore, the excess money eventually dilutes the market value of all money issued. This is called inflation.

In 1971 the US finally switched to fiat money indefinitely. At this point in time many of the economically developed countries' currencies were fixed to the US dollar, and so this single step meant that much of the western world's currencies became fiat money based.

Following the first Gulf War the president of Iraq, Saddam Hussein, repealed the existing Iraqi fiat currency and replaced it with a new currency. Despite having no backing by a commodity and with no central authority mandating its use or defending its value, the old currency continued to circulate within the politically isolated Kurdish regions of Iraq. It became known as the "Swiss dinar." This currency remained relatively strong and stable for over a decade. It was formally replaced following the Second Gulf War.

## Credit money

Credit money often exists in conjunction with other money such as fiat money or commodity money, and from the user's point of view is indistinguishable from it. Most of the western world's money is credit money derived from national fiat money currencies. In a modern economy, a bank will lend to borrowers in excess of the reserve it carries at any time, this is known as fractional reserve banking. In doing so, it increases the total money supply above that of the total amount of the fiat money in existence (also known as M0). While a bank will not have access to sufficient cash (fiat money) to meet all the obligations it has to depositors if they wish to withdraw the balance of their check accounts (credit money), the majority of transactions will occur using the credit money (checks and electronic transfers).

Strictly speaking a debt is not money, primarily because debt cannot act as a unit of account. All debts are denominated in units of something external to the debt. However, credit money certainly acts as a substitute for money when it is used in other functions of money (medium of exchange and store of value).

## Social evolution

Money is an invention of the human mind. The creation of money is made possible because human beings have the capacity to accord value to symbols.

Money is a symbol that represents the value of goods and services. The acceptance of any object as money – be it wampum, a gold coin, a paper currency note or a digital bank account balance – involves the consent of both the individual user and the community. Thus, all money has a psychological and a social as well as an economic dimension. As human society has evolved, the nature and function of money has evolved too.

While a history of money may trace the origin and usage of different forms of money at different times and in different parts of the world, an evolutionary perspective on money traces the social and psychological changes in human attitude and collective behavior that made possible this historical development.

## Barter

Before the invention of money, barter was the primary medium of exchange. An individual possessing a material object of value, such as a measure of grain, could directly exchange that object for another object perceived to have equivalent value, such as a small animal, a clay pot or a tool. The capacity to carry out transactions was severely limited since it depended on a coincidence of wants. The seller of food grain had to find a buyer who wanted to buy grain and who also could offer in return something the seller wanted to buy. There was no common medium of exchange into which both seller and buyer could convert their tradable commodities.

There was no standard which could be applied to measure the relative value of various goods and services.

## Commodity money

The first stage in the evolution of money was the acceptance of certain inherently valuable objects, such as metals, cows, goats or food grains, as a common standard of measure and unit of exchange. It was relatively easy for people to accept any of these as money because they had inherent use value for every individual and, therefore, their wide acceptance by other people was assured. All metals were accepted because they could be readily converted into precious tools and weapons, e.g. knives, axes, spears and spades. Gold and silver had secondary advantages. They were also easy to identify and visually attractive. Gold, silver, copper as well as other usable material objects such as salt and peppercorns are categorized as commodity money, since they combine the attributes both of a usable commodity and a symbol. People accepted foods and metals as money because they were sure of their value to themselves and to other people.

The introduction of metal coins marked a step or bridge in the evolution from usable commodities to symbolic forms of money. Although metal had a use value of its own, coins were accepted in trade for their symbolic value as a medium and standard measure for exchanging other goods and services of value rather than for utilization of the metal they contained.

The term commodity money is also applied to other objects of less obvious utility such as shells, beads and stones, whose utilitarian value was only decorative. This classification tends to blur an important distinction between money consisting of usable commodities and pure symbolic money.

## Representative money

The next stage in the evolution of money involved a further transition from money as an object with inherent usefulness and value to money as a pure symbol of value. Representative money is symbolic money that is based on useful commodities. This category includes the warehouse receipts issued by the ancient Egyptian grain banks, the goldsmith receipts issued by England's goldsmith bankers, bills of exchange based on tradable goods, and more recent forms of paper currency that were backed by and redeemable for gold or silver. The adoption of representative money represented a significant evolution in human consciousness. Psychologically, the individual had to transfer the sense of value from a usable material object to an abstract symbol. Socially, groups of people had to agree on the common usage of the same symbol.

## Warehouse receipts

Warehouse receipts became a very successful form of representative money in ancient Egypt during the reign of the Ptolemies around 330 BC.

Farmers deposited their surplus food grains for safe-keeping in royal or private warehouses and received in exchange written receipts for specific quantities of grain. The receipts were backed and redeemable for a usable commodity. Being much easier to carry, store and exchange than bags of grain, they were accepted in trade as a secure and more convenient form of payment, acting as a symbolic substitute for the quantities of food grain they represented. The warehouse receipt itself had no inherent value. It was only a symbol for something of value.

The invention of representative money had profound effect on the evolution of both money and society. It directly led to the creation of a new social organization, banking. The network of royal and private banks that were created during the reign of the Ptolemies constituted a national grain or giro-banking system. Grains were deposited in 'banks' for safekeeping. Warehouse receipts were accepted as a form of symbolic money because they were fully 'backed' by the grains in the warehouse.

More importantly but less obviously, the introduction of banking by the Pharaohs of Egypt made possible the creation of money. Until then new money could be grown as a crop, raised as an animal or discovered as metal in the earth. Now it could be created by writing a warehouse receipt. At first these receipts were issued only when additional grain was deposited and cancelled whenever the grain was withdrawn from the warehouse.

But it required only a small step in imagination for the bankers to realize that they could also create new grain receipts on other occasions. If someone applied to the bank for financial assistance, the bank did not need to provide it in the form of grain. It could simply create and give to the borrower a new warehouse receipt that was indistinguishable from those issued when grain was deposited. Although the new receipts were not backed by additional deposits of grain, they were still backed by the total value of grain on deposit at the warehouse and, therefore, readily accepted in the market as a medium of exchange, so long as the public had trust and confidence in the overall financial strength of the grain bank.

This stage marks a crucial transition from money as a thing to money as a symbol of trust. In the case of commodity money, trust was placed in the inherent value of the metal or grain which constituted the form of payment. In the case of the warehouse receipt, trust was extended from the commodity to the social organization that held the grain and issued the receipts. This shift required a psychological willingness on the part of the individual to accept a symbol in place of a physical object and a social willingness on the part of the collective to evolve organizations and systems of account that could gain and hold the public trust.

These ancient girobanks went even further. They introduced standardized accounting methods and bank accounts for their depositors.

Deposits could be recorded as numerical entries in their books of account. Large transfers of money from one account holder to another could be done without even exchanging warehouse receipts, simply by changing the account balances in the bank's record books. The number in the record book became a symbolic form of representative money, an ancient forerunner of modern electronic forms of money.

## Tallies

The acceptance of symbolic forms of money opened up vast new realms for human creativity. A symbol could be used to represent something of value that was available in physical storage somewhere else in space, such as grain in the warehouse. It could also be used to represent something of value that would be available later in time, such as a promissory note or bills of exchange, a document ordering someone to pay a certain sum of money to another on a specific date or when certain conditions have been fulfilled. In the 12th Century, the English monarchy introduced an early version of the bill of exchange in the form of a notched piece of wood known as a tally stick. Tallies originally came into use at a time when paper was rare and costly, but their use persisted until the early 19th Century, even after paper forms of money had become prevalent. The notches were used to denote various amounts of taxes payable to the crown. Initially tallies were simply used as a form of receipt to the tax payer at the time of rendering his dues.

As the revenue department became more efficient, they began issuing tallies to denote a promise of the tax assessee to make future tax payments at specified times during the year. Each tally consisted of a matching pair – one stick was given to the assessee at the time of assessment representing the amount of taxes to be paid later and the other held by the Treasury representing the amount of taxes be collected at a future date. The Treasury discovered that these tallies could also be used to create money. When the crown had exhausted its current resources, it could use the tally receipts representing future tax payments due to the crown as a form of payment to its own creditors, who in turn could either collect the tax revenue directly from those assessed or use the same tally to pay their own taxes to the government.

The tallies could also be sold to other parties in exchange for gold or silver coin at a discount reflecting the length of time remaining until the taxes was due for payment. Thus, the tallies became an accepted medium of exchange for some types of transactions and an accepted medium for store of value. Like the girobanks before it, the Treasury soon realized that it could also issue tallies that were not backed by any specific assessment of taxes. By doing so, the Treasury created new money that was backed by public trust and confidence in the monarchy rather than by specific revenue receipts. [9]

## Trade Bills of Exchange

Bills of exchange became prevalent with the expansion of European trade toward the end of the Middle Ages. A flourishing Italian wholesale trade in cloth, woolen clothing, wine, tin and other commodities was heavily dependent on credit for its rapid expansion. Goods were supplied to a buyer against a bill of exchange, which constituted the buyer's promise to make payment at some specified future date. Provided that the buyer was reputable or the bill was endorsed by a credible guarantor, the seller could then present the bill to a merchant banker and redeem it in money at a discounted value before it actually became due. These bills could also be used as a form of payment by the seller to make additional purchases from his own suppliers. Thus, the bills – an early form of credit – became both a medium of exchange and a medium for storage of value. Like the loans made by the Egyptian grain banks, this trade credit became a significant source for the creation of new money. In England, bills of exchange became an important form of credit and money during last quarter of the 18th century and the first quarter of the 19th century before banknotes, checks and cash credit lines were widely available. [10]

## Goldsmith bankers

The highly successful ancient grain bank also served as a model for the emergence of the goldsmith bankers in 17th Century England.

These were the early days of the mercantile revolution before the rise of the British Empire when merchant ships began plying the coastal seas laden with silks and spices from the orient and shrewd traders amassed huge hoards of gold in the bargain. Since no banks existed in England at the time, these entrepreneurs entrusted their wealth with the leading goldsmith of London, who already possessed stores of gold and private vaults within which to store it safely, and paid a fee for that service. In exchange for each deposit of precious metal, the goldsmiths issued paper receipts certifying the quantity and purity of the metal they held on deposit. Like the grain receipts, tallies and bills of exchange, the goldsmith receipts soon began to circulate as a safe and convenient form of money backed by gold and silver in the goldsmiths' vaults.

Knowing that goldsmiths were laden with gold, it was only natural that other traders in need of capital might approach them for loans, which the goldsmiths made to trustworthy parties out of their gold hoards in exchange for interest. Like the grain bankers, goldsmith began issuing loans by creating additional paper gold receipts that were generally accepted in trade and were indistinguishable from the receipts issued to parties that deposited gold. Both represented a promise to redeem the receipt in exchange for a certain amount of metal. Since no one other than the goldsmith knew how much gold he held in store and how much was the value of his receipts held by the public, he was able to issue receipts for greater value than the gold he held.

Gold deposits were relatively stable, often remaining with the goldsmith for years on end, so there was little risk of default so long as public trust in the goldsmith's integrity and financial soundness was maintained. Thus, the goldsmiths of London became the forerunners of British banking and prominent creators of new money. They created money based on public trust.

## Banknotes

The history of money and banking are inseparably interlinked. The multiplication of money really took off when banks got into the business. Inspired by the success of the London goldsmiths, some of which became the forerunners of great English banks, banks began issuing paper notes quite properly termed " banknotes" which circulated in the same way that government issued currency circulates today. In England this practice continued up to 1694. Scottish banks continued issuing notes until 1850. In USA, this practice continued through the 19th Century, where at one time there were more than 5000 different types of bank notes issued by various commercial banks in America. Only the notes issued by the largest, most creditworthy banks were widely accepted. The script of smaller, lesser known institutions circulated locally. Farther from home it was only accepted at a discounted rate, if it was accepted at all. The proliferation of types of money went hand in hand with a multiplication in the number of financial institutions.

These banknotes were a form of representative money which could be converted into gold or silver by application at the bank. Since banks issued notes far in excess of the gold and silver they kept on deposit, sudden loss of public confidence in a bank could precipitate mass redemption of banknotes and result in "bankruptcy." The use of bank notes issued by private commercial banks as legal tender has gradually been replaced by the issuance of bank notes authorized and controlled by national governments. The Bank of England was granted sole rights for the issuance of banknotes in England after 1694. In the USA, the Federal Reserve Bank was granted similar rights after its establishment in 1913. Until recently, these government-authorized currencies were forms of representative money, since they were partially backed by gold or silver and convertible into metal under certain circumstances.

## Demand deposits

The primary business of the grain and goldsmith bankers was safe storage of savings. The primary business of the early merchant banks was promotion of trade. The new class of commercial banks made accepting deposits and issuing loans their principal activity. They lend the money they received on deposit. They created additional money in the form of new bank notes. They also created additional money in the form of demand deposits simply by making numerical entries in the ledgers of their account holders.

The money they created was partially backed by gold, silver or other assets and partially backed only by public trust in the institutions that created it.

## Gold-backed banknotes

For most of us, the term gold standard is erroneously thought to refer to a time when currency notes were fully backed by and redeemable in an equivalent amount of gold. The British pound was the strongest, most stable currency of the 19th Century and often considered the closest equivalent to pure gold, yet at the height of the gold standard there was only sufficient gold in the British treasury to redeem a small fraction of the currency then in circulation. In 1880, US government gold stock was equivalent in value to only 16% of currency and demand deposits in commercial banks. By 1970, it was about 0.5%. The gold standard was only a system for exchange of value between national currencies, never an agreement to redeem all paper notes for gold. The classic gold standard prevailed during the period 1880 and 1913 when a core of leading trading nations agreed to adhere to a fixed gold price and continuous convertibility for their currencies. Gold was used to settle accounts between these nations. With the outbreak of World War I, Britain was forced to abandon the gold standard even for their international transactions. Other nations quickly followed suit. After a brief attempt to revive the gold standard during the 1920s, it was finally abandoned by Britain and other leading nations during the Great Depression.

Prior to the abolition of the gold standard, the following words were printed on the face of every US dollar: "I promise to pay the bearer on demand, the sum of one dollar" followed by the signature of the US Secretary of the Treasury. Other denominations carried similar pledges proportionate to the face value of each note. The currencies of other nations bore similar promises too. In earlier times this promise signified that a bearer could redeem currency notes for their equivalent value in gold or silver. The US adopted a silver standard in 1785, meaning that the value of the US dollar represented a certain equivalent weight in silver and could be redeemed in silver coins. But even at its inception, the US Government was not required to maintain silver reserves sufficient to redeem all the notes that it issued. Through much of the 20th Century until 1971, the US dollar was 'backed' by gold, but from 1934 only foreign holders of the notes could exchange them for metal.

## Fiat money

Since 1971 the US dollar is not backed by anything. It is pure fiat money. The promise was quietly withdrawn and currency notes no longer carry that pledge. The same is true of all major currencies in the world today. This marks the final stage in the evolution of pure fiat money which is neither backed by a commodity nor convertible into a commodity. Fiat money has become the standard form of national currency since abandonment of the gold standard.

Banknotes issued by private banks were backed by the total deposits of the banks that issued them, however inadequate those deposits might be to reimburse all depositors. Notes issued by the US Federal Reserve or other central banks are backed only by the perception of public confidence in the stability of government and the productive capacity of the country that issues them. The transition from bank notes to government-guaranteed currency marks the evolution from trust in a financial institution to trust in the economic capacity and future prosperity of the nation. The greater a country's production and productivity, the more the goods and services it offers in exchange for legal tender, and therefore the greater the confidence and trust in that currency. That is a major reason why the value of the euro has risen as the European Union had expanded to include more countries with greater productive capacity.

In the United States, the history of money has expressed a powerful and fascinating story. The Federal Reserve Bank of San Francisco in its 1995 report published some very interesting explanations on the history of money and its role in modern American life. This is what is mentioned in its website in terms of reference to money:

In our society today, money's value is measured by what it can buy--its purchasing power--not by its material worth, but it hasn't always been so.

American currency has spanned centuries of evolution and numerous transfigurations to reach the size and shape that we carry in our wallets today. It has been an evolutionary process, which often came about in times of crisis--like the Civil War or Great Depression--or to respond to demand as society struggled to put into place a monetary system that would function smoothly and inspire confidence. This development process is ongoing and continues even now as redesigned is issued in 1996. But the legacy of the process is a rich heritage of United States currency that gives us a fascinating, colorful, and reflective glimpse into the growth of our nation.

The Federal Reserve Bank has a special interest in this subject. As part of our role as the government's central bank we are responsible for putting currency, as well as coin, into circulation. Indeed, the warehousing, shipping, processing, and handling of currency are major functions of the regional Reserve banks.

## Colonial and Continental Currency

The Massachusetts Bay Colony issued the first paper money in the colonies in 1690. Other colonies soon followed suit to meet the high demand for money fueled by trade between the colonies and the scarcity of coin (which was the common form of money up to this date). Some of this early money was readily accepted, but some was not redeemed in gold or silver as promised and thus depreciated rapidly.

These currencies, however, set a precedent for the first national currency, which was issued during the War for Independence.

To finance the Revolutionary War, the Continental Congress in 1775 authorized the limited issuance of paper currency. These notes, called Continentals, were denominated in dollars and backed by the "anticipation" of future tax revenues, with no backing in silver or gold. They could be redeemed only upon the independence of the colonies.

Continentals were an interesting expression of the new nation's sovereignty, as they did not feature pictures of the crown or King of England. In fact, some were printed from plates engraved by Paul Revere to read "The United Colonies" and bore pictures of colonial minutemen.

Without solid backing and with rising inflation, the Continentals soon became worthless, thus the expression "not worth a Continental." Or, as George Washington put it, "A wagonload of currency will hardly purchase a wagonload of provisions."

In 1777 after the Declaration of Independence was signed, the first notes bearing the words "The United States" were issued and signed by well-known revolutionary figures to give them credibility.

The remnant of this experience was a deep distrust of paper money, which was not issued again by the federal authorities until the Civil War when the Federal government first issued paper money. The Continental was significant, however, in that it marked the first time that the worth of U.S. currency lay in its purchasing power and not in its intrinsic value.

## Free Banking Era

In 1791 the Bank of the United States received a charter to operate until 1811, followed by the Second Bank of the United States from 1816 to 1836. These two banks, chartered by Congress rather than a state, performed several central bank functions. Although privately owned, they were authorized to issue paper bank notes and serve as the fiscal agent of the government.

Both banks, however, were unpopular with those wanting easy credit--primarily the western, agrarian interests-- and in 1832 Andrew Jackson vetoed the recharter of the Second Bank.

Thus followed the "Free Banking Era"--a quarter century in which American banking was a hodgepodge of state-chartered banks with no federal regulation or uniformity in operating laws. State Bank notes of various sizes, shapes, and designs were in circulation.

Some of them were relatively safe and exchanged for par value and others were relatively worthless as speculators and counterfeiters flourished. By 1860, an estimated 8,000 different state banks were circulating "wildcat" or "broken" bank notes in denominations from ½ cent to $20,000. The nickname "wildcat" referred to banks in mountainous and other remote regions that were said to be more accessible to wildcats than customers, making it difficult for people to redeem these notes. The "broken" bank notes took their name from the frequency with which some of the banks failed, or went broke.

## Civil War

Once again the need to finance a war provided the impetus for a change in the monetary system. In 1861, to finance the Civil War, Congress authorized Demand Notes--the first issue of paper money by the government since the Continentals. These Notes were printed in $5, $10, and $20 denominations, redeemable in coins on demand, and green in color--hence the name "greenbacks." A total of about $10 million was issued, a relatively small series. These notes, and all paper money issued since 1861, are still valid and redeemable in current cash at face value. While most early money is now in the hands of collectors or museums, it is important to note the record of currency stability, which this represents.

In 1862, Congress discontinued issuing Demand Notes and issued Legal Tender Notes, also known as United States Notes. These new notes--issued in denominations from $1 to $1,000 (later $5,000 and $10,000)--were the first national currency used as legal tender for most public and private debts. The design of these notes incorporated a Treasury seal, fine-line engraving, intricate geometric lathe work patterns, and later incorporated various forms of distinctive cotton and linen papers with embedded red and blue fibers. Confidence in the notes waned somewhat when the Treasury stopped redeeming them in coins during the Civil War to save gold and silver. However, redemption resumed in 1879 following the war.

Coin hoarding and the need to use metals for war purposes created a shortage of coin during the Civil War and led to the circulation of small change substitutes. In some cases these included tickets, bills, and even postage stamps.

From 1862 to 1876 the government issued more than $368 million in Fractional Currency in three-to fifty-cent denominations. These "paper coins," which were much smaller in size than our present currency, were nicknamed "shinplasters," as the hardships of war often forced troops to line their worn-out boots with them. These fractional notes are still redeemable today.

Between 1861 and 1865 Confederate currency was being issued to millions of Southerners, gambling that a Confederate victory would ensure the currency would be redeemable. In an effort to debase this currency, the North printed counterfeit Confederate money and circulated it in the south. Inflation was soon rampant in both the north and south, but far worse in the Confederacy. As the end of the war neared, Confederate citizens completely lost confidence in their currency and came to rely on barter or black-market greenbacks. In some cases Confederate soldiers were even paid in Northern greenbacks. By the end of the war, Confederate notes were totally worthless.

## National Bank Act

President Abraham Lincoln, urged by the Secretary of the Treasury, convinced Congress to pass the National Banking Act of 1863, which established a national banking system and a uniform national currency to be issued by the new "national banks." The banks were required to purchase U.S. government securities as backing for their National Bank Notes. In 1865 a 10-percent tax was levied on State Bank notes eliminating the profit in issuing them and basically taxing them out of existence.

Although United States Notes were still widely accepted as a medium of exchange, most paper currency circulating between the Civil War and World War I consisted of National Bank Notes.

They were issued from 1863 through 1932. From 1863 to 1877 National Bank Notes were printed by private bank note companies under contract to the Federal government. The Federal government took over printing them in 1877.

GOLD AND SILVER CERTIFICATES

The economy was in turmoil in the late 19th century. The government, in a move to increase its reserve of precious metals, offered certificates in exchange for deposits of silver and gold.

Gold certificates, colorful and vivid, were first issued in 1863 and put into general circulation in 1882. They are among the most attractive of all currency issues, with the reverse a brilliant golden orange, symbolic of the gold coin they represent. In 1933, when the country faced a severe depression and a banking crisis, the public began to demand gold.

Runs developed on both Federal Reserve Banks (which had been established under the Federal Reserve Act in 1913) and commercial banks. In order to deal with this crisis, only Federal Reserve Banks were permitted to hold gold. In 1934, Federal Reserve Banks were required to turn over all gold coin, bullion, and certificates to the U.S. Treasury in return for a new type of gold certificate. These were never put into circulation and the last ones were printed in January 1935.

In 1964, private citizens could once again hold gold certificates issued before January 30, 1934, but they could no longer be redeemed in gold. This changed in 1974, and private U.S. citizens could once again hold gold legally.

In 1913 a major change in paper currency occurred with the passage of the Federal Reserve Act aimed at resolving some long-standing money and banking problems which had led to bank failures, business bankruptcies, and general economic contractions. The Act created the Federal Reserve System as the nation's central bank to regulate the flow of money and credit for economic stability and growth. In 1914, Federal Reserve Notes, which comprise more than 99 percent of today's paper money, were issued by Federal Reserve Banks as direct obligations of the Federal Reserve System. They replaced National Bank Notes as the dominant form of paper money.

## The Bretton Woods system

After World War 2 an international system was designed to aid in the reconstruction of all nations. This was done by setting a system of fixed foreign currency exchange rates between nations. The actual agreement was hammered out in an American resort in Bretton woods.

This Bretton Woods arrangement did two things;

1) It set up a mutually agreed upon exchange rate between nations and
2) The dollar was pegged at a conversion of one oz. of gold $=\$35US$

What this system did was to indirectly define the value of each world currency in terms of gold. As America expanded post WW2, there was great demand nationally for foreign goods. America was importing more goods than it was exporting. This resulted in massive trade deficits. This created a danger if any foreign nation wanted conversion of their credits in gold since the amount of gold in the US was finite. Richard Nixon, a president of the United States, decided that it would make sense to get the US off the gold standard. So, in 1971 he decided to get the country out of the gold standard. This meant that the US kept all the gold in its treasuries and did not use gold as a medium of exchange for measuring foreign debts. This resulted in a defacto devaluation of the US currency and a movement of trade and business away into a fiat currency.

## Fiat currency and inflation

A fiat currency meant that the dollar value was based on the faith and pledge of the United States Government and had no relationship with any backing of the currency in gold.

This created an incentive for overprinting of currency notes by the Federal Reserve to finance budget deficits and trade deficits. As more and more paper money was in circulation compared to the amounts of goods and services produced this was an immediate recipe for inflation. As long as growth of money in circulation exceeded the growth of production of goods and services, inflation kept creeping into the economy.

Inflation then represented an eating up of the value of the dollar and represented a subtle tax on the citizen's earnings. Hence money in the form of fiat currency steadily lost its purchasing value, one of the factors, which caused the great global financial and credit crisis.

CONCLUSION

This chapter talks about the origin, growth and evolution of money. Money is represented both as a medium of exchange and a storehouse of value. This dual significance has stayed with us even today although the physical form of money has changed from being "commonly accepted shells and coins" through change to "commodity money" to finally becoming a fiat currency.

Money has national and international significance and represents accepted conversion values. By this I mean, that society and governments and markets determine what is worth how much and how resources get allocated inside an economy to produce different goods and services.

Inside a country the politically ordained and accepted currency is the nationally acknowledged paper note--- however in the form of trade and services globally money operates through an international market set system of exchange rates. These exchange rates are meant to indicate the value or lack of value of a nation's currency---however this exchange system is not always accurate due to great manipulated by currency traders like the large banks, financial institutions and global speculators.

Money only derives its meaning from its accepted power to buy goods and services and overprinting of currency notes often creates inflationary pressures. This result in money losing its purchasing value and represents an indirect hidden tax to the country's citizens.

Banking and fiat money are the latest trends today. Since banks have become such great intermediaries of capital their behavior affects the value of money both inside a national system and also within the global financial system. The global financial system can be viewed as a system within which different countries trade with each other. If a country lives within its budget responsibly and creates a credit in its external trade business then it represents a financially advanced nation. In terms of trade development and expansion, this requires trade financing, an area in which banks have become very active.

Within a national boundary, the concept of money derives its value from the ability of a citizen to tap into it (money) by way of a variety of loans. If a businessman wants to expand his business, he needs to borrow money from again, a bank. If a private citizen wants to buy a car or a house or do some unexpected shopping he again needs to take a loan. In a sophisticated economy like the US, credit has become a very important ingredient of health of the economy and money system. However, banks are the dominant intermediaries who gather and invest public capital and if such banks become unhealthy then by default the credit system becomes clogged. A clogged credit system leads to general unavailability of capital, which reflect itself in less business expansion and less expenditure for goods and services. This results sooner or later in unemployment and low consumer spending. This results in economic growth being stifled and such conditions lead to recession and lack of consumer and business confidence. These represent the conditions in which we have found ourselves in the United States as a result of vigorous devious and criminal activities by banks.

To close, money is an invention of the mind. Since money in today's world is only backed by the faith and resources of a Government and country, it is easy to see how a global crisis of this magnitude results in no one trusting their money with no one else--- a situation which breeds conflict, pain and lack of economic and national progress.

To have money flowing easily in the system in the form of credit, to have bank's controlled and regulated to vigorously with a view to serving the public and national need, to see people getting back to work and the economy humming is really the goal of any economy in the world and to which purpose this book is committed.

## Notes

1. ^ Sheila C. Dow (2005), "Axioms and Babylonian thought: a reply", *Journal of Post Keynesian Economics* **27** (3), p. 385-391.
2. ^ http://history-world.org/reforms_of_urukagina.htm
3. ^ *Charles F. Horne, Ph.D. (1915).* "The Code of Hammurabi : Introduction" *(in English). Yale University.* http://www.yale.edu/lawweb/avalon/medieval/hammint.htm. Retrieved on September 14 2007.
4. ^ Shells are believed to be 100,000-year-old jewelry - 6/23/2006 8:12:00 AM - JCK-Jewelers Circular Keystone
5. ^ http://rg.ancients.info/lion/article.html Goldsborough, Reid. "World's First Coin"
6. ^ "Sir Isaac Newton's state of the gold and silver coin (25 September 1717).". Pierre Marteau. http://www.pierre-marteau.com/editions/1701-25-mint-reports/report-1717-09-25.html.

7. ∧ "Mineral Profiles" *(PDF)*. U.S. Geological Survey. http://pubs.usgs.gov/of/2002/of02-303/OFR_02-303.pdf.
8. ∧ Davies, Glyn, ''A History of Money'', University of Wales, 1994, p.51.
9. ∧ Davies, Glyn, ''A History of Money'', University of Wales, 1994, p.146-151.
10. ∧ Davies, Glyn, ''A History of Money'', University of Wales, 1994, p.172, 339.

## References

- Davies, Glyn, History of Money from Ancient Times to the Present Day
- Jevons, W. S. (1875), Money and the Mechanism of Exchange, London: Macmillan.
- Menger, Carl, "On the Origin of Money"
- Szabo, Nick, Shelling Out -- The Origins of Money
- United States Mint
- Royal Mint
- American Numismatic Association
- World Bank

# CHAPTER 6

## THE DUTCH TULIP BUBBLE OF 1636

We now start the historical process of understanding what excesses in financial markets are, why they are caused and how they end. Excesses in one form or other cause bubbles, which result in over exaggeration of asset prices.

So let us start our discovery process in one of the earliest bubbles in modern history---the tulip bubble of 1636.The scene is Holland, one of the growing and enterprising nations in Europe. With great difficulty and stress, this country had just demanded and forced its freedom from Spain and is now trying to grow its economy and people. If you have not been to Holland, I would strongly encourage a trip to that part of the world. It is one of the most beautiful countries in Europe. The Dutch have always been an open and happy people.

Going back to our story in seventeenth century Holland, the tulip was not known as one of their homegrown flowers. The tulip, however, was first introduced in the Netherlands (Holland) in the mid-sixteenth century. It arrived from Constantinople, which was then of the Turkish Ottoman Empire. The Flemish botanist, Charles de L'Ecluse was doing research at the University of Leiden and had requested some tulip bulbs from Constantinople. These bulbs arrived in Leiden, courtesy of the Emperor's Ambassador to the Sultan.

Charles de L'Ecluse now planted these imported bulbs into his garden for the purpose of conducting plant research. These bulbs bloomed into beautiful tulips. Charles's neighbors and associates wanted to purchase some of these bulbs but the botanist was uncomfortable doing this---- this refusal resulted in the neighbors taking the law in their hands by quietly stealing a large portion of these bulbs and propagating and developing them in different plantations and gardens in Holland. In time, due to their beautiful looks, such bulbs became very popular in Holland and were much sought after as collector items and showpieces. They became a luxury item and were especially coveted by the rich. The tulips came in many brilliant colors, starting from the basic white to yellow and red. But it was the multicolored ones, which were most sought after and which commanded the highest prices.

With greater purchasing interest in these bulbs from France, speculation started in this new bulb market. The speculation was primarily in three exotic varieties of tulips, which were in short supply and consequent increasing demand. This demand was generated by the wealthy merchants and business people in Holland. The bulbs took several months to flower into tulips and therefore people contracted to buy them months before they bloomed--- this was the start of the futures market in tulips. Sellers and buyers would meet informally and enter into a contract to purchase/sell the tulips with a delivery date several months into the future, corresponding with the flowering season of the bulbs.

Futures prices for tulips started rising in 1636, finally crashing at the peak of the bubble in 1637. During this speculative period, the prices were bid up dramatically by speculators. Common citizens got into these bidding wars, which resulted in a lot of investors making money as a result of buying these contracts and subsequently selling the same contracts at a higher price in the future. The situation got so crazy that people were contracting to sell their homes, provide thousands of tones of cheese and sell cows and sheep in exchange for the opportunity to obtain a few of the priceless tulips. But this speculative fever could not go on forever. The start of the burst in this marketplace occurred when one of the buyers in 1637 failed to pay for the contracted flowers. This marked the very beginning of the end of this speculative market as new investors now felt that there was diminishing future value in these contracts. As a result very few new contracts were written. Prices now started crashing to the floor as more and more defaults in honoring these futures contracts happened. The bursting of the tulip bubble resulted in untold misery and financial pain for ordinary Dutch citizens.

## MORAL OF THE STORY

What seems so difficult to understand is how something so simple and ephemeral as a tulip flower could command such price volatility. What made the Dutch, known to be a proud, independent and rational people, to stoop to buying and selling flowers at astronomical prices, giving away their homes, their cattle's and their very source of livelihood in exchange for these flowers?

The motivating factor, in one simple word, was greed. The tulip bulbs and flowers by themselves had no great economic or monetary value. It was the fact that everyone else was doing it (the herd mentality) and the explosive rice in prices made even the simple common man risk his money and home and livelihood to get a piece of the great Dutch dream. Greed with its disastrous consequences is the common thread, which will be expressed, in all the historical crises in this book. The Dutch tulip bubble was the first of many world financial crises, which shook the foundations of the Dutch economy and impacted negatively (financially) the Dutch citizen.

# CHAPTER 7

## THE SOUTH SEA BUBBLE OF 1720

The South Sea Bubble was a story of massive speculation involving manipulation of the shares of the South Sea Company. The South Sea Company was established as a British joint stock company. The company's initial mandate was to engage in trading activities in South America during the eighteen century. In 1711, with the blessings of the English royalty and ruling politicians, this company was provided a monopoly by the English Government to trade in Spain's South American colonies.

BACKGROUND

England had spent a lot of money fighting wars with the French and Spanish. During this process it incurred massive national debt, which was becoming difficult to finance from the Exchequer. In order to shift the national debt burden ( and risk  to a recognizable and acceptable third-party, politicians and royalty alike approved the idea of creating a new stock company to which such national deficit risk could be transferred. Thus the new South Sea Company was officially formed.

South Sea Company was a British joint stock company that traded in South America during the eighteenth century.

Founded in 1711, the company was granted a monopoly to trade in Spain's South American colonies as part of a treaty during the War of Spanish Succession. In return for being granted such trade monopoly the South Sea Company assumed the national debt England had incurred during the war. The British Government cleverly convinced their existing debt holders to transfer their existing Government debt to the newly formed South Sea Company in exchange for earning a fixed rate of interest on the new South Sea Debt and an opportunity to earn trading profits by this new monopolistic trade venture. The debt holders of the British Government now became shareholders of the South Sea Company. The Government in one masterful stroke was able to transfer a huge portion of its wartime debt to this newly formed company, in exchange for payment of a "piddly" amount of interest.

Speculation of the South Sea Company stock led to a great economic bubble, known as the South Sea Bubble in 1720, which caused financial ruin to many. In spite of this negative financial occurrence the Company was restructured and continued to operate for more than a century after the bubble.

The South Sea Company was established in 1711 by the Lord Treasurer, Robert Harley. At that time, when continental America was being explored and settled, Europeans applied the term, "South Seas," only to South America and surrounding waters, and not to any other ocean.

The trading rights were presupposed on the successful conclusion of the War of Spanish Succession, which did not end until 1713, but the actual treaty granted rights were not as comprehensive as Harley had originally hoped. Harley needed to provide a mechanism for funding government debt incurred in the course of that war. However, he could not establish a bank, because the charter of the Bank of England made it the only joint stock bank. He therefore established what, on its face, was a trading company, though its main activity was in fact the funding of government debt. In return for its exclusive trading rights the Government saw an opportunity for profitable trade-off. The government and the company convinced the holders of around 10 million British pound sterling of short-term government debt to exchange it with a new issue of stock in the South Sea Company. In exchange, the government granted the company a perpetual annuity from the government paying 576,534 pounds annually on the company's books, or a perpetual loan of 10 million pounds paying around 6% annual interest. This guaranteed the new equity owners a steady stream of earnings to this new venture. The government thought it was a win-win situation because it would fund the interest payment by placing a tariff on the goods brought from South America.

The Treaty of Utrecht of 1713 granted the company the right to send one trading ship per year, the Naïve de Premise (though this was in practice accompanied by 'two tenders"), as well as the Ascent, the contract to supply the Spanish colonies with slaves.

The company did not undertake a trading voyage to South America until 1717 and made little actual profit. Furthermore, when ties between Spain and Britain deteriorated in 1718 the short-term prospects for the company were very poor. Nonetheless, the company continued to argue that its longer-term future would be extremely profitable.

## Debt for equity

In 1717 the company took on a further 2 million pounds of public debt. The rationale in all these transactions was to the

- Government: lower interest rate on its debt.
- South Sea Company (owners): a steady stream of earnings.
- Government debt-holder: an upside potential in a promising enterprise.

## Slave trading

Most commentary on the South Sea Company focuses on the money lost by English investors. The primary trading business of the company was the forced transportation of people purchased in West Africa and then selling them into slavery in the Americas. In fact, the most important aspect of the Company's monopoly trading rights to the Spanish Empire was the 1713 Treaty of Utrecht's slave-trading "Ascent", which granted the exclusive right to sell slaves in all of the American colonies.

The Ascent set a quota of selling 4800 people into slavery a year. Despite its problems with speculation, the South Sea Company was relatively successful at slave trading and meeting its quota.

According to records compiled by David Elytis and others, during the course of 96 voyages in twenty-five years, the South Sea Company purchased 34,000 slaves of whom 30,000 survived the voyages across the Atlantic. * 1

The mortality of about 11% was low for a ship participating in the middle passage and indicates that the organization was an efficient slave trader. Employees, directors and investors overcame major obstacles in order to pursue the slave trade, including two wars with Spain and the 1720 bubble. The company sold its largest number of slaves during the 1725 trading war, five years after the bubble burst.

## Trading more debt for equity

In 1719 the company proposed a scheme by which it would buy more than half the national debt of Britain (around 31 million pounds) again with new shares, and a promise to the government that the debt would be converted to a lower interest rate, 5% until 1727 and 4% per year, thereafter. The purpose of this conversion was similar to the old one. It would allow a conversion of high-interest but difficult-to-trade debt into low-interest, readily marketable debt and shares of the South Sea Company. All parties could gain.

In summary, the total government debt in 1719 was 50 million pounds. This debt was held by:

(i) Bank of England--- 34  million pounds
(ii) British East India Company—3.2 million pounds
(iii) South Sea Company---11.7 million pounds
(iv) Privately held redeemable debt-16.5 million pounds
(v)  Irredeemable annuities of 15 million pounds

The Bank of England proposed a similar competing offer, which did not prevail when the South Sea raised its bid to 7.5 million pounds (plus approximately 1.3 million pounds in bribes). The proposal was accepted in a slightly altered form in April 1720. The Chancellor of the Exchequer, John Aislabie, was a strong supporter of the scheme.

Crucial in this conversion was the proportion of holders of irredeemable annuities that could be tempted to convert their securities at a high price for the new shares. (Holders of redeemable securities had no other choice but to subscribe) The South Sea Company could set the conversion prices but could obviously not diverge much from the market price of its shares.

The company ultimately acquired 85% of the 'redeemables' and 80% of the 'irredeemables.' The company then set to talking up its stock with " the most extravagant rumors" of the value of its potential trade in the New World which was followed by a wave of " speculating frenzy." The share price had risen from the time the scheme was proposed: from 128 pounds in January 1720 to 175 pounds in February, to 330 pounds in March and, following the scheme's acceptance, to 550 pounds at the end of May.

What may have supported the company's high multiples (its P/E) was a fund of credit (known to the market) of 70 million pounds available for commercial expansion, which had been made available through substantial support, apparently, by Parliament and King.

Shares in the company were " sold" to politicians at the current market price; however, rather than paying for the shares, these lucky recipients simply held on to what shares they had been offered, "sold " them back to the company when and as they chose, and received as "profit" the increase in market price. This method, while winning over the heads of government, the King's mistress, etc., also had the advantage of binding their interests to the interests of the company: in order to secure their own profits, they had to help drive up the stock. Meanwhile, by publicizing the name of their elite stockholders, the company managed to clothe itself in an aura of legitimacy, which attracted and kept other buyers.

### Bubble Act

In June 1720, the Royal Exchange and London Assurance Corporation Act of 1719(repealed in 1825) required all joint stock companies to have a Royal Charter. This became known as the Bubble Act later, after the speculative bubble had burst. The grant of a charter to South Sea Company was an added boost, its shares leaping to 890 pounds in early June.

This peak encouraged investors to sell; to counterbalance this company's directors ordered their agents to buy, which succeeded in propping up the price to 750 pounds.

The price of the stock went up over the course of a single year from about one hundred pounds a share to almost one thousand pounds per share. Its success caused country wide frenzy as all types of people--- from peasants to lords----developed a feverish interest in investing; in South Seas primarily, but in stocks generally. Among the many companies to go public in 1720 is--- famously-one that advertised itself as "a company for carrying out an undertaking of great advantage, but nobody to know what it is." *2

The price finally reached 1000 pounds in early August and the level of selling was such that the price started to fall, dropping back to 100 pounds per share before the year was out. This triggered bankruptcies amongst those who had bought on credit, and increased selling, even short-selling (selling borrowed shares in hope of buying them back a profit if the price falls).

By the end of September the stock had fallen to 150 pounds. The company failures now extended to banks and "goldsmiths" as they could not collect loans made on the stock, and thousands of individuals were ruined (including many members of the aristocracy). With investors outraged, Parliament was recalled in December and an investigation began.

Reported in 1721, it revealed widespread fraud amongst the company directors and corruption in the Cabinet.

Among those implicated were John Aislabie,(the Chancellor of the Exchequer),James Craggs the Elder (the Postmaster General), James Craggs the Younger (the Southern Secretary). Aislabie was imprisoned.

The newly appointed first Lord of the Treasury, Robert Walpole was forced to introduce a series of measures to restore public confidence. Under the guidance of Walpole, Parliament attempted to deal with the financial crisis. The estates of the directors of the Company were confiscated and use to relieve the suffering of the victims and the stock of the South Sea Company was divided between the Bank of England and the East India Company. A resolution was proposed in parliament that bankers be tied up in sacks filled with snakes and tipped into the Murky Thames. *3 The crisis significantly damaged the credibility of the King and of the Whig Party.

MORAL OF THE STORY

The incredible South Sea Company saga was an incident of magnificent greed and manipulation. At the center of this scandal were the politicians elected by the people to rule the constituency. Ably assisting these corrupt politicians were the aristocracy themselves. The motivating factor behind this tale of deception was the motivating need of the English exchequer to transfer a significant portion of the national debt to the Company at a very negligible cost. What a marvelous feat of financial engineering!!!

This marvel was far greater than the fraud perpetrated by the investment and commercial banks of the US hundreds of years later in 2007.

The South Sea bubble was a bubble of massive proportions involving great risk and speculations. Again, it got its encouragement from the ruling politicians in England and was supported byte well established banking community. The motivating factor overall in this scenario was greed and the successful attempt at fraudulent risk transference by the Government. As prices of the South Sea stock continued to rise many ordinary people jumped in to buy shares, only to find that they were holding shares, which were pretty worth next to nothing at the end of the company's share price collapse. People lost homes, were declared bankrupt and lost their reputations permanently as a result of this crash. Even goldsmiths and bankers were not spared financially. The Chancellor of the Exchequer was sent to prison for his role in this massive manipulation.

In closing, share price manipulation assisted by bankers, who finance the stock market trade and politicians who sent up the legal framework for companies to operate is a difficult situation to countervail. The moral of the story again is for investors to be very cautious when any stock price or asset price is rising at an astronomical pace. In such situations, it would be wiser not to engage in stock market trading of such specific stocks, however compelling the reasons might appear to purchase such stock.

REFERENCES:

*1   www.historycooperative.org

*2   Charles Mackay: "Extraordinary Popular Delusions and the Madness of Crowds p.65 and 71(Harriman House Classics 2003)

*3 Tied up in a sack of snakes and tipped into Thames.

# CHAPTER 8

# ADAM SMITH AND HIS IMPACT ON THE

# US FINANCIAL SYSTEM

## ADAM SMITH AND THE WEALTH OF NATIONS:

## CHALLENGING PHILOSOPHY IN DIFFICULT FINANCIAL TIMES

**Adam Smith** was a Scottish moral philosopher and a pioneer of political economy. One of the key figures of the Scottish Enlightenment, Smith is the author of *"The Theory of Moral Sentiments"* and *"An Inquiry into the Nature and Causes of the Wealth of Nations."* The latter, usually abbreviated as *The Wealth of Nations*, is considered his *magnum opus* and the first modern work of economics. Adam Smith is widely cited as the father of modern economics.[1][2]

Smith studied moral philosophy at the University of Glasgow and Oxford University. After graduating he delivered a successful series of public lectures at Edinburgh, leading him to collaborate with David Hume during the Scottish Enlightenment. Smith obtained a professorship at Glasgow teaching moral philosophy, and during this time wrote and published " *The Theory of Moral Sentiments.*" In his later life he took a tutoring position which allowed him to travel throughout Europe where he met other intellectual leaders of his day.

Smith returned home and spent the next ten years writing *The Wealth of Nations* (mainly from his lecture notes) which was published in 1776. He died in 1790. In 1759, Smith published his first work, *The Theory of Moral Sentiments*. He continued to revise the work throughout his life, making extensive revisions to the final (6th) edition shortly before his death in 1790.[note 2] Although *The Wealth of Nations* is widely regarded as Smith's most influential work, it has been reported that Smith himself "always considered his *Theory of Moral Sentiments* a much superior work to his *Wealth of Nations*".[57] P. J. O'Rourke, author of the commentary *On The Wealth of Nations* (2007), has agreed, calling *Theory of Moral Sentiments* "the better book".[58] It was in this work that Smith first referred to the "invisible hand" to describe the apparent benefits to society of people behaving in their own interests.[59]

In *The Theory of Moral Sentiments*, Smith critically examined the moral thinking of the time and suggested that conscience arises from social relationships.[60] His aim in the work is to explain the source of mankind's ability to form moral judgments, in spite of man's natural inclinations toward self-interest. Smith proposes a theory of sympathy in which the act of observing others makes people aware of them and the morality of their own behavior. Haakonssen writes that in Smith's theory,

"Society is ... the mirror in which one catches sight of oneself, morally speaking."[61]

In part because *Theory of Moral Sentiments* emphasizes sympathy for others while *Wealth of Nations* famously emphasizes the role of self interest, some scholars have perceived a conflict between these works. As one economic historian observed: "Many writers, including the present author at an early stage of his study of Smith, have found these two works in some measure basically inconsistent."[62] But in recent years most scholars of Adam Smith's work have argued that no contradiction exists. In *Theory of Moral Sentiments*, Smith develops a theory of psychology in which individuals seek the approval of the "impartial spectator" as a result of a natural desire to have outside observers sympathize with them. Rather than viewing the *Wealth of Nations* and *Theory of Moral Sentiments* as presenting incompatible views of human nature, most Smith scholars regard the works as emphasizing different aspects of human nature that vary depending on the situation. The *Wealth of Nations* draws on situations where man's morality is likely to play a smaller role—such as the laborer involved in pin-making—whereas the *Theory of Moral Sentiments* focuses on situations where man's morality is likely to play a dominant role among more personal exchanges.

*The Wealth of Nations* expounds that the free market, while appearing chaotic and unrestrained, is actually guided to produce the right amount and variety of goods by a so-called "invisible hand".[59] The image of the invisible hand was previously employed by Smith in *Theory of Moral Sentiments,* but it has its original use in his essay, "The History of Astronomy". Smith believed that when an individual pursues his self-interest, he indirectly promotes the good of society: "by pursuing his own interest, [the individual] frequently promotes that of the society more effectually than when he intends to promote it."[63] Self-interested competition in the free market, he argued, would tend to benefit society as a whole by keeping prices low, while still building in an incentive for a wide variety of goods and services. Nevertheless, he was wary of businessmen and argued against the formation of monopolies. An often-quoted passage from *The Wealth of Nations* is:[64]

It is not from the benevolence of the butcher, the brewer, or the baker that we expect our dinner, but from their regard to their own self-interest. We address ourselves, not to their humanity but to their self-love, and never talk to them of our own necessities but of their advantages.

Value theory was important in classical theory. Smith wrote that the "real price of every thing ... is the toil and trouble of acquiring it" as influenced by its scarcity. Smith maintained that, with rent and profit, other costs besides wages also enter the price of a commodity.[65]

Other classical economists presented variations on Smith, termed the 'labour theory of value'. Classical economics focused on the tendency of markets to move to long-run equilibrium.

Adam Smith's advocacy of self-interest based economic exchange did not, however, preclude for him issues of fairness and justice. In Asia, Europeans "by different arts of oppression..have reduced the population of several of the Moluccas,"[66] he wrote, while "the savage injustice of the Europeans" arriving in America, "rendered an event, which ought to have been beneficial to all, ruinous and destructive to several of those unfortunate countries."[67] The Native Americans, "far from having ever injured the people of Europe, had received the first adventurers with every mark of kindness and hospitality." However, "superiority of force" was "so great on the side of the Europeans, that they were enabled to commit with impunity every sort of injustice in those remote countries."[68]

Smith also believed that a division of labour would effect a great increase in production. One example he used was the making of pins. One worker could probably make only twenty pins per day. However, if ten people divided up the eighteen steps required to make a pin, they could make a combined amount of 48,000 pins in one day. However, Smith's views on division of labour are not unambiguously positive, and are typically mis-characterized.

Smith says of the division of labor:

"In the progress of the division of labour, the employment of the far greater part of those who live by labour, that is, of the great body of the people, comes to be confined to a few very simple operations, frequently only one or two. ...The man whose whole life is spent in performing a few simple operations, of which the effects too are, perhaps, always the same, or very nearly the same, has no occasion to exert his understanding, or to exercise his invention in finding out expedients for removing difficulties which never occur. He naturally loses, therefore, the habit of such exertion, and generally becomes as stupid and ignorant as it is possible for a human creature to become. ...His dexterity at his own particular trade seems, in this manner, to be acquired at the expense of his intellectual, social, and martial virtues. ...this is the state into which the laboring poor, that is, the great body of the people, must necessarily fall, unless government takes some pains to prevent it."[69]

On labor relations, Smith noted "severity" of laws against worker actions, and contrasted the masters' "clamor" against workers associations, with associations and collusions of the masters which "are never heard by the people" though such actions are "always" and "everywhere" taking place:

"We rarely hear, it has been said, of the combinations of masters, though frequently of those of workmen.

But whoever imagines, upon this account that masters rarely combine, is as ignorant of the world as of the subject. Masters are always and everywhere in a sort of tacit, but constant and uniform, combination, not to raise the wages of labour above their actual rate...Masters, too, sometimes enter into particular combinations to sink the wages of labour even below this rate. These are always conducted with the utmost silence and secrecy till the moment of execution; and when the workmen yield, as they sometimes do without resistance, though severely felt by them, they are never heard of by other people" In contrast, when workers combine, "the masters..never cease to call aloud for the assistance of the civil magistrate, and the rigorous execution of those laws which have been enacted with so much severity against the combination of servants, laborers, and journeymen."[70]

*"The Wealth of Nations"*, one of the earliest attempts to study the rise of industry and commercial development in Europe, was a precursor to the modern academic discipline of economics. In this and other works, Smith expounded how rational self-interest and competition can lead to economic prosperity and well-being. It also provided one of the best-known intellectual rationales for free trade and capitalism, greatly influencing the writings of later economists. Smith was ranked #30 in Michael H. Hart's list of the most influential figures in history,[71] and he is often cited as the father of modern economics.[72]

George Stigler attributes to Smith the central proposition of mainstream economic theory, namely that an individual will invest a resource, for example, land or labour, so as to earn the highest possible return on it. Consequently, all uses of the resource should yield a risk-adjusted equal rate of return; otherwise resource reallocation would result. As a symbol of free market economics Smith has been celebrated by advocates of free market policies as the founder of free market economics, a view reflected in the naming of bodies such as the Adam Smith Institute, Adam Smith Society[88] and the Australian Adam Smith Club,[89] and in terms such as the Adam Smith necktie.[90]

Alan Greenspan argues that, while Smith did not coin the term *laissez-faire*, "it was left to Adam Smith to identify the more-general set of principles that brought conceptual clarity to the seeming chaos of market transactions". Greenspan continues that *The Wealth of Nations* was "one of the great achievements in human intellectual history".[91] P. J. O'Rourke describes Adam Smith as the "founder of free market economics".[92]

However, other writers have argued that Smith's support for laissez-faire has been overstated. Herbert Stein wrote that the people who "wear an Adam Smith necktie" do it to "make a statement of their devotion to the idea of free markets and limited government", and that this misrepresents Smith's ideas.

Stein writes that Smith "was not pure or doctrinaire about this idea. He viewed government intervention in the market with great skepticism ... yet he was prepared to accept or propose qualifications to that policy in the specific cases where he judged that their net effect would be beneficial and would not undermine the basically free character of the system. He did not wear the Adam Smith necktie." In Stein's reading, "*The Wealth of Nations,*" could justify the Food and Drug Administration, The Consumer Product Safety Commission, mandatory employer health benefits, environmentalism, and "discriminatory taxation to deter improper or luxurious behavior".[93]

Similarly, Vivienne Brown stated in *The Economic Journal* that in the 20th century United States, Reaganomics supporters, *The Wall Street Journal*, and other similar sources have spread among the general public a partial and misleading vision of Adam Smith, portraying him as an "extreme dogmatic defender of laissez-faire capitalism and supply-side economics".[94] In fact, *The Wealth of Nations* includes the following statement on the payment of taxes:

"The subjects of every state ought to contribute towards the support of the government, as nearly as possible, in proportion to their respective abilities; that is, in proportion to the revenue which they respectively enjoy under the protection of the state."[95]

Noam Chomsky has argued[note 3] that several aspects of Smith's thought have been misrepresented and falsified by contemporary ideology, including Smith's reasons for supporting markets and Smith's views on corporations. Chomsky argues that Smith supported markets in the belief that they would lead to equality, and that Smith opposed wage labor and corporations.[96] Economic historians such as Jacob Viner regard Smith as a strong advocate of free markets and limited government (what Smith called "natural liberty") but not as a dogmatic supporter of laissez-faire.[97]

The National Post in an article of July 2008 made the following comments about the incredible contributions of Adam Smith:

"One parodic view of Smith is that, as the father not only of economics but of perpetually demonized capitalism, he had no sympathy for those below plinth level. Nothing could be farther from the truth. Smith was very much concerned with improving the lot of ordinary people. In The Wealth of Nations, he pointed to the remarkable social -- and international -- benefits of self-interested interaction through trade and the division of labour. He noted that participants appeared to be guided by an "Invisible Hand" to produce a good that was "no part of their intention." This truism has been the centerpiece of attacks on the capitalist system as motivated by "greed" and "selfishness" and thus morally indefensible.

But the merely obvious observation that Smith's famous "butcher, brewer and baker" are serving us primarily in their own interests in no way detracts from the value of that service, nor implies that they are rendered heartless by their business dealings.

One oft-repeated criticism of Smith is that his insights could not possibly apply to a world of supermarkets and giant corporations, of automobiles and air travel, of global financial institutions and the Internet, of alleged resource depletion and worsening pollution. But despite the fact that politicians and activists persist in biting the Invisible Hand, it continues its remarkable work. More fundamentally, Smith's insights remain valid because he was not merely a supporter of markets and a critic of overweening governments, but also a student of human nature. Indeed, Vernon Smith has pointed out that Adam Smith should also perhaps be known as the "father of psychology." While The Wealth of Nations permeates economics, modern scholarship has still not caught up with many of the remarkable insights of Smith's "other" book, The Theory of Moral Sentiments, which received an unlikely boost earlier this year when it was commended by billionaire philanthropist Bill Gates."

Here is what James Otteson reported in a brilliant article in Volume 50, Issue 11 of the Freeman: Ideas on Liberty:

"Adam Smith was not solely an economist, though that is almost exclusively how he is known today. His Inquiry into the Nature and Causes of the Wealth of Nations (WN) is one of the most important books in the Western tradition. Aside from ushering in the modern market-based economic order, which to varying extents has become the worldwide norm, WN laid out several of the fundamental elements of what has become standard economic theory. The crucial importance of the division of labor, the dependence of specialization on the extent of the available market, the dynamic relation between supply and demand that sets prices, and the generally salutary effects of free trade are all notions that students learn in their first economics class. These topics are all investigated systematically for the first time in Smith's book.

The argumentative strategy of WN is simple: given the way these elemental factors operate, we should expect that material prosperity will vary indirectly with governmental regulation of the marketplace (the less governmental interference, the greater the prosperity); and when one looks at the historical record—which Smith does in enormous and awesome detail—our expectations are in fact borne out.[1] WN's conclusion, then, is in the form of a hypothetical imperative: if we want increasing material prosperity, we must decrease governmental interference in the operations of marketplaces.

WN was published in 1776, and the subsequent history of the nations that adopted Smith's recommendations to the greatest extent—America and England—would seem to have vindicated his argument: no place in the world has seen as much increase in material prosperity, before or since, as post-1776 America and England.[2] Because of its enormous historical influence and the corroboration of its central tenets, then, Smith's Wealth of Nations has rightfully earned for itself a central place in the canon of great works of the Western tradition.

Smith became quite famous in both Britain and on the continent during his lifetime, but, perhaps surprisingly, not so much for the Wealth of Nations. Rather, it was for his earlier book, first published in 1759, on ethics. The Theory of Moral Sentiments (TMS) was written during an extraordinarily active period in ethical thought. Francis Hutcheson, who founded the so-called sentimentalist school of ethics, was Smith's teacher; David Hume was Smith's best friend and intellectual sparring partner; and Immanuel Kant, who read Smith carefully, was about to come onto the scene. It is no exaggeration to say that Smith's book was able not only to synthesize the important theoretical work done before him, but also to set the program for ethical philosophy for at least a generation after he died in 1790. Since about the middle of the nineteenth century, however, when Smithian economics began to make influential converts, WN has eclipsed TMS in recognition, readership, and, hence, influence.

I think that the inattention to Smith's first book has been a mistake. TMS is a sufficiently subtle and sophisticated book to merit serious scholarly attention even absent its great influence on moral philosophy during the eighteenth century. Indeed, TMS has another asset that recommends it: as is the case with WN, its argument is, in its essentials, sound. Let me summarize the argument here, then, in the hopes that you will come to see Smith not merely as an economist, but as Smith saw himself, something perhaps grander: a moral philosopher.

## Acquiring Moral Standards

Smith's goal in TMS is to discover by means of empirical investigation the process that explains two phenomena: on the one hand, the adoption by individuals of moral standards by which they judge others; and, on the other, their adoption of moral standards by which they judge themselves. One striking feature about both phenomena is that during their lifetime's people seem to go from having virtually no such standards as children to having standards that are commonly shared with others as adults. What explains this transition?

Smith argues that all human beings innately have something he called a desire for "mutual sympathy" of sentiments. What Smith means is that each of us gets pleasure on seeing his own sentiments echoed in others.

It gives us pleasure when, for example, our friends find the same things funny that we do, to the same degree, or we find the same things distasteful as our friends do, to the same degree. Smith thinks it is simply a fact about human nature that we find this mutual accord, or concordance of sentiments—what Smith terms "sympathy"—pleasurable. (And note, incidentally, Smith's special use of the term "sympathy": it means harmony or concord with any emotion whatsoever; it does not mean only pity or compassion.) In fact, he thinks this pleasure is one of the finest that human beings experience.

Since everyone finds this pleasurable, everyone seeks it out; and this mutual seeking-out of sympathy of sentiments becomes, for Smith, the engine of social cohesion and the centripetal force, as it were, of human communities. It encourages people not only to enter into groups, alliances, and communities with others (so that they have opportunities to achieve the much-sought-after mutual sympathy of sentiments), but also to form associations of like-minded people (because this increases the chances of actually achieving such a sympathy).

The mechanism, Smith thinks, is this: I desire mutual sympathy of sentiments with you, which leads me to moderate my sentiments to the level that I think, based on my past experience, you are likely to "enter into." You, on the other hand, because you desire the same thing, also moderate your sentiments to the level you think, based on your past experience, I am likely to enter into.

Over time this process trains our sentiments to gravitate toward mutually acceptable levels. Smith's picture thus has a clear anti-Freudian thrust: it denies the hydraulic picture of human emotions according to which emotions build up "pressure" that must be "released." Instead, and more plausibly, it conceives of emotions as things that can be controlled and trained by exercising what Smith calls "self-command." The activity of reciprocal adjustment is then repeated numberless times in every person's lifetime, as it is between and among the people in one's community, resulting in the creation of an unintended and largely unconscious system of standards. These standards then become the rules by which we determine in any given case what kind of behavior is, as Smith calls it, "proper" in a situation and what "improper"—meaning what others can reasonably be expected to enter into.

Think of a person laughing too long at a joke: at some point you start to form the judgment that his laughter is simply too much; you judge it, that is, to be "improper." But how do you know at what point the laughing becomes too much? According to Smith, you know by judging this case against the standards you have unintentionally, and probably unconsciously, developed in conjunction with the members of your community over time. In different situations, the amount of laughter that is acceptable may differ; but in each case our experience with our fellows in similar situations sets the parameters for our judgment of propriety.

The same holds true with attire: there is such a thing as dressing inappropriately—in either direction, as it were: wearing black tie to a beach party, or wearing a bathing suit to a wedding—and your judgment of when a person's attire becomes inappropriate is a function of the mechanism Smith describes. To take a final example, there is even, Smith thinks, such a thing as too little anger. If a man's wife is being publicly humiliated by another man, then we think he ought to show anger, or what Smith calls "spirit." If he does not—if he cowers, without rising to her defense—then we judge him to have acted improperly. The propriety or impropriety of a person's behavior, then, is constituted by its accordance or discordance with what is recommended by this system of standards.

To facilitate our ability to predict what our own behavior should be (that is, what would enjoy mutual sympathy with others), Smith thinks we learn to adopt the standpoint of an "impartial spectator" from which to judge our own behavior. He believes that in time we come to take the impartial spectator's judgments as the standard of morality—first for ourselves and then also for others. We have all experienced the unpleasantness of being judged unfairly, that is, on the basis of biased or incomplete information (people who do not know our situation thinking poorly of us). This leads us to desire that others refrain from judging until they know the whole story; but because we all want this, our desire for mutual sympathy of sentiments subtly encourages us to adopt an outside perspective, as it were, in judging our own conduct.

That is, because we want others to be able to "enter into" our sentiments, we strive to moderate them to be what we think others will sympathize with; but we can only know what that is if we ask ourselves what the impartial observer would think. The voice of the impartial spectator becomes our second-nature guide of conduct. Indeed, Smith thinks it is what we call our "conscience." The phrase "let your conscience be your guide" really means to let the imagined impartial spectator be your guide. And because we come to rely on this impartial spectator to give us accurate moral guideposts by which to judge our own behavior, our confidence in his judgments leads us also to employ him to judge others. In this way the impartial spectator becomes the standard of morality.

Let me summarize Smith's explanation of the process of developing moral standards. Babies have only desires; they have no tincture of remorse, shame, or guilt at desiring something improper. As they grow into children, however, they have the first experience of discipline, which teaches them that others judge them and expect them to behave in particular ways. And they make the shocking, arresting discovery that they are not the most important person in everyone's life—only in their own. Their desire for mutual sympathy then encourages them to discover what others expect of them and to strive to achieve it. The more experience they have, the better they become at anticipating others' expectations and hence of behaving in ways that lead to mutual sympathy.

The children then develop habits of behavior that reflect what they have learned; what were once rules handed down from on high become internalized principles by which the children routinely order their lives.

As adults, larger and larger experience leads to more and more complicated, internalized principles. These principles now cover a large range of actions and motivations, and they have been revised, corrected, and fine-tuned as necessary. The principles inform Smith's procedure of making moral judgments: they are the standard against which people judge themselves and others. They are what, in practice, render the moral judgment. A moral judgment, then, is the result of a deduction by which one determines whether a given act or motivation accords with these principles.

**Institutional Theory**

Smith's analysis of the way in which people and communities come to have common moral standards is intriguing—and, indeed, may in large part be true. This alone would recommend it for serious consideration. But Smith's examination of human morality reveals a model for explaining the development and maintenance of large-scale human institutions generally—which would mean that the book's import is yet greater than initially thought. I call Smith's model a "marketplace model." Let me sketch it briefly, drawing on the discussion so far.

First, Smith argues that moral judgments, along with the rules by which we render them, develop in the way I have described, without an overall, pre-arranged plan. They arise and grow into a shared, common system of morality—a general consensus regarding the nature of virtue, or what Smith calls propriety and merit—on the basis of countless individual judgments made in countless particular situations.

Second, Smith argues that as we grow from infants to children to adults we develop increasingly sophisticated principles of action and judgment, which enable us to assess and judge an increasingly diverse range of actions and motivations.

Third, what seem when we are children to be isolated and haphazard interactions with others lead as we grow older to habits of behavior; as adults the habits solidify into principles that guide what we call our "conscience."

Fourth, people's interests, experiences, and environments change slowly enough to allow long-standing associations and institutions to arise, which give a firm foundation to the rules, standards, and protocols that both set the parameters for the initial creation of these associations and in turn are supported by them. (These "associations" would today include everything from Elks clubs, YMCAs, and Boy Scouts, to the American Medical Association, the National Academy of Sciences, and even the Catholic Church.)

Smith next argues that the development of personal moral standards, of a conscience and the impartial spectator procedure, and of the accepted moral standards of a community all depend on the regular associations people make with one another. It is in these associations, in the daily intercourse people have with one another, that they encourage each other to discover and adopt rules of behavior and judgment that will lead to mutual sympathy. Without such interactions with others, Smith argues, people would have no occasion to pursue such rules, and hence they would not. In that case moral judgments would not be made at all, and people would not, as a Robinson Crusoe would not, have thoughts about virtue or vice, propriety, or impropriety. (Smith, in fact, speaks of a "solitary islander," who, with no "societal mirror" by which to view his actions, does not think of the virtue or vice of his actions—just as he would not think about the "beauty or deformity" of his physical appearance.)

Finally, a person's (largely unconscious) adoption of general rules, development of a conscience, and employment of the impartial spectator procedure are motivated by a fundamental, innate desire—the desire for mutual sympathy. This desire is the sine qua non for Smith's theory of moral sentiments: without it, there would have been no reason to devise rules that enable people to achieve it, and, on Smith's theory, there would therefore have been no moral standards at all.

The model at work in TMS, then, comprises four central structural features: a system of order arising unintentionally from the actions of individuals (Smith was the first person to develop and work out the notion of what Hayek made famous two centuries later as "spontaneous order"), an unconscious and slow development of rules by which the system operates, the system's dependence on regular exchange among freely associating people, and a system that receives its initial and ongoing impetus from the desires of the people who make use of it. These four central features of Smith's account are, I would like to suggest, also the central characteristic features of an economic market. We can, then, accurately view Smith's conception of the system of interactions in which moral standards develop as a marketplace of morals.[3]

## Other Marketplaces

By calling Smith's model a "marketplace" model, I already suggest in what way Smith's analysis can explain areas of human life outside of moral judgment-making. The first and most obvious application is to economic marketplaces, where the model Smith sets out in TMS matches up perfectly. Another application is to the human institution of languages. In an early essay titled "Considerations Concerning the First Formation of Languages," Smith lays out how he suspects languages first came into being and how they change over time. The processes he describes in that essay are instances of the processes he set out at greater length in TMS, and his model for language change foreshadows in important ways contemporary theories about language change[4]—a remarkable feat considering that linguistics was only in its infancy at the time. In fact, the three areas of morality, economics, and linguistics can be mapped onto one another quite nicely in terms of the four central features I listed above:

- **Motivating Desire**

1. TMS: the "pleasure of mutual sympathy" of sentiments;
2. WN: the "natural effort of every individual to better his own condition";
3. "Languages": the desire to make our "mutual wants intelligible to each other."

- **Rules Developed**

1. TMS: rules determining propriety and merit;
2. WN: protocols protecting private property, contractual agreements, and voluntary exchanges;
3. "Languages": rules of grammar, pronunciation, and so on.

- **Market (medium or arena of exchange)**

1. TMS: mutual exchange of personal sentiments and moral judgments;
2. WN: exchange of private goods and services;
3. "Languages": verbal communication.

- **Resulting "Unintended System of Order"**

1. TMS: commonly shared standards of morality and moral judgment;
2. WN: economy (large-scale network of exchanges of goods and services);
3. "Languages": language.

I can now suggest why Smith's analysis in TMS is of general applicability: the model it constructs for explaining the development of moral standards can be fruitfully employed to understand not only the development of morality, economic markets, and languages, but indeed the development of all human social institutions. It can, for example, account for the accepted protocols of behavior in a fifteenth-century Indian bazaar as well as those of late-twentieth-century American business; it can explain why certain forms of address and speech are peculiarly acceptable among academic professors, on the one hand, and among inner-city gang members, on the other; it can explain why Americans think the English are stuffy and why the English think Americans are loose.

Smith's model is thus extraordinarily powerful, and its scope may be coterminous with the whole of human social activity itself. This is not to say that the model as Smith presents it is perfect or flawless. One possible problem is its almost exclusive reliance on the desire for mutual sympathy of sentiments: although this desire may well be a foundational element of human nature, it seems clear that there are also other motivating desires. Thus one might object that Smith's picture of human motivation may be too simplistic. On the other hand, I see no reason to think that a richer view of the range of human motivation would necessarily be incompatible with the formal elements of Smith's model. As long as people still strive to satisfy the desires that motivate them, and as long as the satisfaction of those desires requires the presence and sometime cooperation of others, Smith's model would still seem to hold.

Another possible problem is that the moral standards that develop in the way Smith describes would not seem to have any ultimate sanction—they would seem justified, that is, solely because their peculiar historical course of social interaction produced them. That would seem to imply a cultural moral relativism that many—including me—find distasteful. It is a disputed point among Smith scholars whether he in fact thought that moral judgments had any kind of transcendent justification.

I think the fact that they issue from natural human desires and needs begins to lend them objectivity, as does Smith's claim that these "natural" desires and needs were implanted in us by God—which would mean that the moral standards that unintentionally arise by their operation actually reflect the will of God.

Some scholars maintain, however, that Smithian moral standards, like the standards of etiquette, are simply a matter of convention driven by their relative utility at satisfying local, contingent, or changing desires. But I would point to what Smith actually said, and it seems to me that human nature is enough of a constant to anchor a "middle-way" objectivism—between personal subjectivism and absolutely transcendent objectivism—that is sufficient to answer most worries about relativism.

Smith's Theory of Moral Sentiments is thus full of far-reaching possibilities. One astonishing surprise is that, although published exactly 100 years before Darwin's Origin of Species in 1859, TMS's examination of the way in which these systems of unintended order, as I call them, develop and change over time adumbrates in substantial part the way in which Darwin's theory explains the development and change of species.

If recent work in what is called "sociobiology"—the field of inquiry that attempts to explain large parts of human social behavior by employing evolutionary insights[5]—has merit, then Smith's TMS, which is the first book in the Western tradition to try to work out such a view, might well have been on to something important indeed.

Thus The Theory of Moral Sentiments has had enormous historical influence, is subtle and sophisticated, develops an account of morality that is plausible and persuasive, and works out a model for explaining human interaction that is powerful enough to encompass virtually the entire range of human life. On top of that, some recent empirical research suggests his theory might be true. I can think of little else a book would need to be included as one of the greatest works of the Western tradition. I therefore commend it to you for your consideration, and I hope you will think of Smith not merely as an economist, but rather as he thought of himself: a moral philosopher. []

---

**Notes**

1. For contemporary evidence substantiating Smith's Landes, The Wealth and Poverty of Nations: Why Some Are So Rich and Some Are So Poor (New York: Norton, 1999).

2. For further discussion of this claim, see James R. Otteson, "Adam Smith's Marketplace of Morals," Archiv für Geschichte der Philosophie (forthcoming).
3. Two examples are Rudi Keller, On Language Change: The Invisible Hand in Language (London: Routledge, 1994) and Steven Pinker, The Language conclusions, see the annually updated Economic Freedom of the World compilation, available at www.freetheworld.com/release.html.
4. For a recent study supporting this claim, see David S.
5. Instinct: How the Mind Creates Language (New York: Harper–Collins, 1995).
6. A classic statement of this view is E. O. Wilson's On Human Nature (Cambridge, Mass.: Harvard University Press, 1978); a more recent treatment that draws explicitly on Smith's work is James Q. Wilson, The Moral Sense (New York: Free Press, 1993)

Notes

1.  ^ *Hoaas, David J.; Madigan, Lauren J. (1999), "A citation analysis of economists in principles of economics textbooks",* The Social Science Journal *36 (3): 525–532,* doi:10.1016/S0362-3319(99)00022-1
2.  ^ Rae 1895, p. 292
3.  ^ Bussing-Burks 2003, pp. 38–39
4.  ^ Buchan 2006, p. 12
5.  ^ [a] [b] [c] Rae 1895, p. 5
6.  ^ [a] [b] [c] Bussing-Burks 2003, p. 39
7.  ^ Buchan 2006, p. 22
8.  ^ Bussing-Burks 2003, p. 41
9.  ^ Rae 1895, p. 24
10. ^ [a] [b] Buchholz 1999, p. 12
11. ^ Introductory Economics. *New Age Publishers. p. 4.* ISBN 8122418309.
12. ^ Rae 1895, p. 22
13. ^ Rae 1895, pp. 24–25
14. ^ [a] [b] Bussing-Burks 2003, p. 42
15. ^ Buchan 2006, p. 29
16. ^ Rae 1895, p. 30
17. ^ [a] [b] Bussing-Burks 2003, p. 43.
18. ^ *Winch, Donald (September 2004). "Smith, Adam (bap. 1723, d. 1790)". Dictionary of National Biography.* Oxford University Press.
19. ^ Rae 1895, p. 42
20. ^ [a] [b] Buchholz 1999, p. 15
21. ^ Buchan 2006, p. 67
22. ^ [a] [b] [c] [d] [e] Buchholz 1999, p. 16
23. ^ Buchholz 1999, pp. 16–17
24. ^ [a] [b] Buchholz 1999, p. 17
25. ^ Buchan 2006, p. 80
26. ^ [a] [b] Buchholz 1999, p. 18
27. ^ Buchan 2006, p. 90
28. ^ Buchholz 1999, p. 19

29. ^ Buchan 2006, p. 89
30. ^ "First Visit to London". Library of Economics and Liberty. http://econlib.org/library/YPDBooks/Rae/raeLS10.html. Retrieved 2008-05-22.
31. ^ Buchan 2006, p. 128
32. ^ Buchan 2006, p. 133
33. ^ Buchan 2006, p. 137
34. ^ Buchan 2006, p. 145
35. ^ *a b* Bussing-Burks 2003, p. 53
36. ^ *a b* Buchan 2006, p. 25
37. ^ *a b* Buchan 2006, p. 88
38. ^ Bonar 1895, p. xx–xxiv
39. ^ Buchan 2006, p. 11
40. ^ Buchan 2006, p. 134
41. ^ Rae 1895, p. 262
42. ^ *a b c* Skousen 2001, p. 32
43. ^ *a b* Buchholz 1999, p. 14
44. ^ *a b* Buchholz 1999, p. 12
45. ^ *Stewart, Dugald (1853). The Works of Adam Smith: With An Account of His Life and Writings. London: Henry G. Bohn. lxix.* OCLC 3226570. http://books.google.com/books?id=FbYCAAAAYAAJ.
46. ^ Rae 1895, pp. 376-377
47. ^ Bonar 1895, p. xxi
48. ^ Ross 1995, p. 15
49. ^ "Times obituary of Adam Smith". *The Times. 1790-07-24.*
50. ^ Coase 1976, pp. 529-546
51. ^ Coase 1976, p. 538
52. ^ "Hume on Religion". Stanford Encyclopedia of Philosophy. http://plato.stanford.edu/entries/hume-religion/. Retrieved 2008-05-26.

53. ^ "Letter From Adam Smith, LL.D. TO William Strahan, Esq. - Essays Moral, Political, Literary (LF ed.)". *Online Library of Liberty*. http://oll.libertyfund.org/?option=com_staticxt&staticfile =show.php%3Ftitle=704&chapter=137475&layout=html &Itemid=27. Retrieved 2008-05-26.
54. ^ Rae 1895, p. 311
55. ^ Buchan 2006, p. 51
56. ^ Adam Smith, Glasgow Edition of the Works and Correspondence Vol. 1 *The Theory of Moral Sentiments* (1759)
57. ^ Rae 1895
58. ^ O'Rourke, P. J. *(2007-01-08).* "P.J. O'Rourke Takes On 'The Wealth of Nations'". NPR. http://www.npr.org/templates/story/story.php?storyId=6 743689. Retrieved 2008-06-10.
59. ^ *ᵃ ᵇ Minowitz, Peter (December 2004).* "Adam Smith's Invisible Hands". Econ Journal Watch *1 (3): 381-412.* http://www.econjournalwatch.org/pdf/MinowitzComme nt1December2004.pdf.
60. ^ *Falkner, Robert (1997).* "Biography of Smith". Liberal Democrat History Group. http://www.liberalhistory.org.uk/item_single.php?item_i d=37&item=biography. Retrieved 2008-05-14.
61. ^ Smith and Haakonssen 2002, p. xv
62. ^ Viner 1991, p. 250
63. ^ Wealth of Nations
64. ^ Smith 1776, p. 18
65. ^ Smith, Adam (1776). The Wealth of Nations, Bk. 1, Ch. 5, 6.
66. ^ Wealth of Nations, Book IV, Chap. vii
67. ^ [http://socserv.socsci.mcmaster.ca/~econ/ugcm/3ll3/smit h/wealth/wealbk04 Wealth of Nations, Book IV, Chap. I.]
68. ^ Wealth of Nations, Book IV, Chap. vii.

69. ^ Wealth of Nations, Book V, Chap. I.
70. ^ Wealth of Nations, Book I. Chap. viii
71. ^ Hart 1989
72. ^ *Pressman, Steven (1999). Fifty Major Economists. Routledge. p. 20.* ISBN 0415134811.
73. ^ Roemer, J.E. (1987). "Marxian Value Analysis". *The New Palgrave: A Dictionary of Economics*, v. 3, 383.
74. ^ Mandel, Ernest (1987). "Marx, Karl Heinrich", *The New Palgrave: A Dictionary of Economics. 3, pp. 372, 376.*
75. ^ *Marshall, Alfred; Marshall, Mary Paley (1879). The Economics of Industry. p. 2.* http://books.google.com/books?hl=en&lr=&id=NLcJAA AAIAAJ&pg=PA1#PPA2,M1.
76. ^ *Jevons, W. Stanley (1879). The Theory of Political Economy (2nd ed.). p. xiv.* http://books.google.com/books?id=aYcBAAAAQAAJ& pg=PR3#PPR3,M1.
77. ^ Clark, B. (1998). *Political-economy: A comparative approach*, 2nd ed., Westport, CT: Preagerp. p. 32..
78. ^ Campos, Antonietta (1987). "Marginalist Economics", *The New Palgrave: A Dictionary of Economics*, v. 3, p. 320
79. ^ Smith 1977, §Book I, Chapter 2
80. ^ *"Clydesdale 50 Pounds, 1981". Ron Wise's Banknote world.* http://aes.iupui.edu/rwise/banknotes/scotland/ScotlandP2 09-50Pounds-1981-donatedowl_f.jpg. Retrieved 2008-10-15.
81. ^ *"Current Banknotes : Clydesdale Bank". The Committee of Scottish Clearing Bankers.* http://www.scotbanks.org.uk/banknotes_current_clydesd ale_bank.php. Retrieved 2008-10-15.
82. ^ *"Smith replaces Elgar on £20 note". BBC. 2006.* http://news.bbc.co.uk/1/hi/business/6096938.stm. Retrieved 2008-05-14.

83. ^ *Blackley, Michael (2007-09-26). "Adam Smith sculpture to tower over Royal Mile". Edinburgh Evening News.*

84. ^ *Fillo, Maryellen (2001-03-13). "CCSU welcomes a new kid on the block". The Hartford Courant.*

85. ^ *Kelley, Pam (1997-05-20). "Piece at UNCC is a puzzle for Charlotte, artist says".* Charlotte Observer.

86. ^ *Shaw-Eagle, Joanna (1997-06-01). "Artist sheds new light on sculpture". The Washington Times.*

87. ^ "Adam Smith's Spinning Top". *Ohio Outdoor Sculpture Inventory. Archived from* the original *on 2005-02-05.* http://web.archive.org/web/20050205065104/http://www.sculpturecenter.org/oosi/sculpture.asp?SID=1055. Retrieved 2008-05-24.

88. ^ *"The Adam Smith Society". The Adam Smith Society. Archived from* the original *on 2007-07-21.* http://web.archive.org/web/20070721032612/http://www.adamsmith.it/presentazione.html. Retrieved 2008-05-24.

89. ^ *"The Australian Adam Smith Club". Adam Smith Club.* http://www.adamsmithclub.org/. Retrieved 2008-10-12.

90. ^ *Levy, David (June 1992). "*Interview with Milton Friedman*". Federal Reserve Bank of Minneapolis.* http://www.minneapolisfed.org/publications_papers/pub_display.cfm?id=3748. Retrieved 2008-09-01.

91. ^ *"FRB: Speech, Greenspan—Adam Smith—6 February 2005".* http://www.federalreserve.gov/boarddocs/speeches/2005/20050206/default.htm. Retrieved 2008-05-31.

92. ^ *"Adam Smith: Web Junkie - Forbes.com".* http://www.forbes.com/free_forbes/2007/0507/086.html. Retrieved 2008-06-10.

93. ^ *Stein, Herbert (1994-04-06). "Board of Contributors: Remembering Adam Smith". The Wall Street Journal Asia: A14.*

94. ^ *Brown, Vivienne (January 1993).* "Untitled review of 'Capitalism as a Moral System: Adam Smith's Critique of the Free Market Economy' and 'Adam Smith and his Legacy for Modern Capitalism'". *The Economic Journal* **103** *(416): 230–232.* doi:*10.2307/2234351.*
95. ^ Adam Smith, The Wealth of Nations: Book V, Chapter II (Of the Sources of the General or Public Revenue of the Society, Part II, Of Taxes; V.2.25)
96. ^ Chapter 6
97. ^ *Viner, Jacob (April 1927).* "Adam Smith and Laissez-faire". *The Journal of Political Economy* **35** *(2): 198–232.* doi:*10.2307/2234351.*

References

- *Bonar, James (1895), A Catalogue of the Library of Adam Smith, London: Macmillan,* OCLC 2320634, http://books.google.com/books?id=pUmfjlAfM3kC
- *Buchan, James (2006),* The Authentic Adam Smith: His Life and Ideas, *W. W. Norton & Company,* ISBN 0393061213.
- *Buchholz, Todd (1999),* New ideas from Dead Economists: An introduction to modern economic thought, *Penguin Books,* ISBN 0140283137.
- *Bussing-Burks, Marie (2003),* Influential Economists, *Minneapolis: The Oliver Press,* ISBN 1-881508-72-2.
- *Campbell, R. H.; Skinner, Andrew S. (1985),* Adam Smith, *Routledge,* ISBN 0709934734.
- Coase, R.H. *(October 1976),* "Adam Smith's View of Man", *The Journal of Law and Economics* **19** *(3): 529–546,* doi:*10.1086/466886*

- Hart, Michael H. *(March 1989), The 100, Carol Publishing Group,* ISBN 0806510684.
- Rae, John *(1895), Life of Adam Smith, New York City: Macmillan Publishers,* ISBN 0722226586, http://books.google.com/books?id=V80JAAAAIAA J&printsec=frontcover&dq=Adam+Smith+-inauthor:%22Adam+Smith%22&ei=lCArSNj3K4u ujgGNgtnCDQ#PPA4,M1.
- *Ross, Ian Simpson (1995-12-14),* The Life of Adam Smith, *Oxford University Press,* ISBN 0198288212.
- Skousen, Mark *(2001), The Making of Modern Economics: The Lives and Ideas of Great Thinkers, M.E. Sharpe,* ISBN 0765604809, http://books.google.com/books?id=nsnl3hHPuowC.
- *Smith, Adam (1776 [1977]),* An Inquiry into the Nature and Causes of the Wealth of Nations, *University Of Chicago Press,* ISBN 0226763749.
- *Smith, Adam (1759 [1982]), The Theory of Moral Sentiments, ed. D.D. Raphael and A.L. Macfie, vol. I of the Glasgow Edition of the Works and Correspondence of Adam Smith, Liberty Fund,* ISBN 0865970122, http://oll.libertyfund.org/index.php?option=com_sta ticxt&staticfile=show.php%3Ftitle=192&Itemid=27 .
- *Smith, Adam (1759 [2002]), Knud Haakonssen, ed., The Theory of Moral Sentiments, Cambridge University Press,* ISBN 0521598478, http://www.cambridge.org/catalogue/catalogue.asp? isbn=0521598478
- *Smith, Vernon L. (July 1998)).* "The Two Faces of Adam Smith". Southern Economic Journal **65** *(1):* 2–19.

- *Tribe, Keith; Mizuta, Hiroshi (2002) (Hardcover),* A Critical Bibliography of Adam Smith*, Pickering & Chatto,* ISBN 9781851967414
- *Viner, Jacob (1991). Douglas A. Irvin. ed.* Essays on the Intellectual History of Economics. *Princeton, New Jersey: Princeton University Press.* ISBN 0691042667.

- *This article incorporates public domain text from:* Cousin, John William (1910). *A Short Biographical Dictionary of English Literature.* London, J. M. Dent & sons; New York, E. P. Dutton.

# CHAPTER 9

## ADAM SMITH RE-VISITED

Adam Smith, a Scottish professor made economic observations more than two centuries ago. The bulk of his theories have been tested through two hundred years of economic results in the US and most of his theories have tested positive. Very simply, Adam Smith preached the virtues of Individual Liberty and Personal Responsibility. He hypothesized 200 years back which truths are self-evident today that individuals operating in a free Society which encouraged individual liberty and justice and gave everyone a level playing field, work-wise would result in great accumulation of national wealth. This is why economic performance has been great in most open, democratic societies, which believe in the equal and just application of Law for their citizens.

Let us look at some other comments by eminent business leaders on the influence and work of Adam Smith. In a speech to the World Congress of Housing Finance, Resident Fellow, Alex J. Pollock on September 20,2006 made the following important comments on Adam Smith's work:

"What is the proper role for the government in the financial system, and in housing finance, in particular? This is among the "essentially contestable questions"--those which may be debated for decades and centuries without clear resolution.

The two dominant theories are respectively derived from two great political economists: Adam Smith and John Maynard Keynes.

In *The Wealth of Nations*, published in the famous year 1776, Smith set the lasting intellectual framework for thinking about the productive power of competitive private markets, which has transformed the world. In this view, government intervention is particularly prone to creating monopolies and special privileges, which generate undeserved monopoly profits (economic rents), constrain competition, and reduce productivity. It thus results in less wealth being created for the society and ordinary people are made worse off.

Keynes, writing amidst the world financial collapse and economic crisis of the 1930s, came to the opposite view: that state intervention was both necessary and beneficial to address problems which markets could not solve on their own.

When financial behavior is dominated by fear and extreme uncertainty, only the compact power of the state, with its sovereign authority to compel, tax and borrow, is available to move things forward.

Considering at length this debate of ideas and prescriptions for political economy, the noted economic historian, Charles Kindleberger, asked, "So should we follow Smith or Keynes?" He concluded that the only possible rational answer is: "*Both, depending on the circumstances.*" In other words, the answer is different at different times.

## A Proposal

Kindleberger was the author (among many other works) of *Manias, Panics and Crashes*, a wide ranging history of the financial busts which follow booms, first published in 1978, and prescient about the financial crises of the following generation. A fifth edition of this book, updated by Robert Z. Aliber, has brought the story up to our more recent dot-com mania and subsequent scandals, to which the same fundamental patterns continue to apply.

Kindleberger, surveying several centuries of financial history, observed that financial crises and scandals occur, on average, about once every ten years. This matches my own experience in banking and finance, which began during the "credit crunch "of 1969, then the collapse of the Penn Central Railroad and the U.S. commercial paper market in the next year, and various other memorable busts since. The most senior representative to the 2006 World Congress of Housing Finance, Howard Sexton, Chairman of the Southern Cross Building Society, New Zealand since the 1960s, has told me that once every ten years matches his experience, too. It seems to take financial actors less than a decade to forget the lessons their predecessors painfully learned.

This pattern gives rise to my proposal for balancing between Smith and Keynes, which expands upon Kindleberger's insight of "Both, depending on the circumstances," by *quantifying* how much we should have of each. Since crises and scandals occur about 10% of the time, the proposed mix is as follows:

*Pollock Proposal*
Adam Smith : 90%, for normal times

J.M. Keynes: 10%, for times of crisis.

In normal times, we want the economic efficiency, innovation, productivity and resulting economic well-being of ordinary people created by competitive private markets. But when the financial system hits its periodic crises, the intervention and coordination of the state can be helpful. This intervention should, however, be temporary. If prolonged, it will tend to monopoly, bureaucracy, less innovation, and less growth. In the extreme, it will become socialist stagnation.

So the Keynesian actions should be temporary. We should have the 90% Smith, 10% Keynes mix, with the state interventions withdrawn after the crisis is over.

This is the *Cincinnatian Doctrine*, modeled after the Roman hero Cincinnatus, who flourished in the fifth century B.C. Cincinnatus became Dictator of Rome, being "called from the plough to save the state." In the classic Roman Republic, the dictatorship was a temporary office, which the holder was expected to resign after the crisis was addressed. Cincinnatus did--and went back to his farm.

Cincinnatus was a model for the American founding fathers and for George Washington, in particular. Washington became the "Modern Cinicinnatus" for saving his country twice, once as General and once as President, and returning to his farm each time.

When he probably could have become King of America after the Revolution, he resigned his command instead. Upon hearing this, George III famously remarked, "If this be true, he is the greatest man of the age!"

But those who attain political and economic power do not often have the virtue of Cincinnatus or Washington. The key problem with this doctrine is therefore: how to get the intervention to withdraw when its time has passed? When monopoly profits, market power, and the bureaucratic interests of government agencies become imbedded in the financial system, how do we return to the proper Smithian competition for the next 90% of the time?

## The American GSEs as an Example

Consider as notable examples of this problem the American Housing "Government-Sponsored Enterprises" (the "GSEs"), a $ 5 trillion sector of the U.S. housing finance system.

Each of the GSEs was created as a response to particular circumstances of a real or perceived crisis in housing finance, in the following years:

| | |
|---|---|
| Fannie Mae | 1938 |
| Federal Home Loan Banks | 1932 |
| Freddie Mac | 1970 |

The existence of each GSE reflected some specific historical moment. Each GSE got government sponsorship with special benefits, privileges and advantages for its shareholders, because it addressed pressing problems for politicians at the time. Every GSE represents a deal made with the government to trade privileges for helping with such problems in line with the Keynesian theory.

It would be astonishing if the circumstances of the time did not change dramatically in the course of several decades--as of course they have. Fannie was created solely to buy FHA-insured mortgages, a function it no longer performs. The Federal Home Loan Banks were created to focus entirely on small, local, mutual savings associations, but their principal customers are now giant interstate banks. Freddie was created to solve the shortage of mortgage credit caused by interest rate ceilings on deposits, but these ceilings were ended two decades ago. In short, none of the circumstances which prompted the creation of any of the GSEs still exists. The original deals are all passé', indeed completely irrelevant.

But these government interventions have not been withdrawn, and all the GSEs are still here, having developed in ways never intended or foreseen by their designers.

They are all huge issuers of debt with the implicit guaranty of the government, of enormous size, financial influence and political importance, and enjoy billions of dollars of economic rents (monopoly profits). They are now very hard to control, the accounting scandals of Fannie and Freddie of recent years notwithstanding.

GSEs are the marriage of government privileges and private benefits, created in crisis for purposes now outmoded. Unlike other marriages, they should always end in divorce--in other words, the Cincinnatian Doctrine should be applied. But how?

## Applying the Cincinnatian Doctrine to the GSEs

The following steps should be taken to move the GSEs in a Cincinnatian direction:

> First of all, abolish their perpetual charters and replace them with limited-life charters of ten years duration. Giving the GSEs perpetual charters was a major mistake. With a limited-life charter, there is at least a regular chance to reconsider the deal with the government and take account of the inevitably changed circumstances.

Foster competition among and for GSEs in all sensible ways. Competition will curtail their market power and economic rents, and increase the probability of ultimate privatization.

Apply the logic that GSEs are in reality joint ventures in partnership with the capital of the government. As former Congressman J. J. Pickle of Texas observed about them, "The risk is 99% public and the profit is 100% private." If this formula were corrected and the profit were divided according to the risk bearing, it would increase the motivation of the GSE managers to pursue privatization.

Clearly target privatization as the goal, once the original crisis has passed.

Insure that all future interventions, in response to the crises of the future, have limited-life charters or sunset provisions.

In short, unlike Cincinnatus, GSEs and other state interventions will not voluntarily go back to private life. They need to be forced.

*An Inquiry into the Nature and Causes of the Wealth of Nations*

*The Wealth of Nations* is, without doubt, a book that changed the world. But it has been taking its time. Two hundred thirty-one years after publication, Adam Smith's practical truths are only beginning to be absorbed in full. And where practical truths are most important — amid counsels of the European Union, World Trade Organization, International Monetary Fund, British Parliament, and American Congress — the lessons of Adam Smith end up as often sunk as sinking in.

## Adam Smith's Simple Principles

Smith illuminated the mystery of economics in one flash: "Consumption is the sole end and purpose of all production." There is no mystery. Smith took the *meta* out of the *physics*. Economics is our livelihood and just that.

*The Wealth of Nations* argues three basic principles and, by plain thinking and plentiful examples, proves them. Even intellectuals should have no trouble understanding Smith's ideas. Economic progress depends upon a trinity of individual prerogatives: pursuit of self-interest, division of labor, and freedom of trade.

There is nothing inherently wrong with the pursuit of self-interest. That was Smith's best insight. To a twenty-first-century reader this hardly sounds like news. Or, rather, it sounds like everything that's in the news. These days, altruism itself is proclaimed at the top of the altruist's lungs. Certainly it's of interest to the self to be a celebrity. Bob Geldof has found a way to remain one. But for most of history, wisdom, beliefs, and mores demanded subjugation of ego, bridling of aspiration, and sacrifice of self (and, per Abraham with Isaac, of family members, if you could catch them).

This meekness, like Adam Smith's production, had an end and purpose. Most people enjoyed no control over their material circumstances or even — if they were slaves or serfs — their material persons. In the doghouse of ancient and medieval existence, asceticism made us feel less like dogs.

But Adam Smith lived in a place and time when ordinary individuals were beginning to have some power to pursue their self-interest. In the chapter "Of the Wages of Labour," in book 1 of *The Wealth of Nations*, Smith remarked in a tone approaching modern irony, "Is this improvement in the circumstances of the lower ranks of the people to be regarded as an advantage or as an inconveniency to the society?"

If, in the eighteenth century, prosperity was not yet considered a self-evidently good thing for the lower ranks of people, it was because nobody had bothered to ask them. In many places nobody has bothered to ask them yet. But it is never a question of folly, sacrilege, or vulgarity to better our circumstances. The question is how to do it.

The answer is division of labor. It was an obvious answer— — except to most of the scholars who had theorized about economics prior to Adam Smith. Division of labor has existed since mankind has. When the original Adam delved and his Eve span, the division of labor may be said to have been painfully obvious. Women endured the agonies of childbirth while men fiddled around in the garden.

The Adam under present consideration was not the first philosopher to notice specialization or to see that divisions are as innate as labors. But Smith was arguably the first to understand the manifold implications of the division of labor. In fact he seems to have invented the term.

The little fellow with the big ideas chips the spear points. The courageous oaf spears the mammoth. And the artistic type does a lovely cave painting of it all. One person makes a thing, and another person makes another thing, and everyone wants everything.

Hence trade. Trade may be theoretically good, or self-sufficiency may be theoretically better, but to even think about such theories is a waste of that intermittently useful specialization, thought. Trade is a fact.

Adam Smith saw that all trades, when freely conducted, are mutually beneficial by definition. A person with this got that, which he wanted more, from a person who wanted this more than that. It may have been a stupid trade. Viewing a cave painting cannot be worth three hundred pounds of mammoth ham. The mutuality may be lopsided. A starving artist gorges himself for months while a courageous oaf of a new art patron stands bemused in the Grotte de Lascaux. And what about that wily spear point chipper? He doubtless took his mammoth slice. But they didn't ask us. It's none of our business.

Why an Inquiry into Adam Smith's Simple Principles Is Not an Inquiry, First, into Adam Smith

Most things that people spend most of their time doing are none of our business. This is a very modern idea. It makes private life — into which we have no business poking our noses — more fascinating than private life was to premoderns. Adam Smith was a premodern, therefore this book is organized in an old-fashioned way. The man's ideas come first. The man comes afterward.

Adam Smith helped produce a world of individuality, autonomy, and personal fulfillment, but that world did not produce him. He belonged to an older, more abstracted tradition of thought.

When a contemporary person's ideas change the world, we want to know about that person. Did Julia Child come from a background of culinary sophistication, or did her mother make those thick, gooey omelets with chunks of Velveeta cheese and Canadian bacon like my mother? I fed them to the dog. What elements of nature and nurture, of psychology and experience, developed Julia Child's thinking? But there was a time when thinking mostly developed from other thinking. The thinkers weren't thinking about themselves, and their audience wasn't thinking of the thinkers as selves, either. Everyone was lost in thought. Dugald Stewart, who in 1858 published the first biography of Adam Smith, excused its scantiness of anecdote with the comment, "The history of a philosopher's life can contain little more than the history of his speculations."

Another reason to put the history of Adam Smith's speculations ahead of the history of Adam Smith is that Smith led the opposite of a modern life — uneventful but interesting. He was an academic but an uncontentious one.

159

He held conventional, mildly reformist political views and would have been called a Whig if he'd bothered to be involved in partisan politics. He became a government bureaucrat. Yet the essence of his thinking — "It's none of our business" — will eventually (I hope) upend everything that political and religious authorities have been doing for ten thousand years. In a few nations the thinking already works. There are parts of the earth where life is different than it was when the first physical brute or mystical charlatan wielded his original club or pronounced his initial mumbo jumbo and asserted his authority in the first place.

The whole business of authority is to interfere in other people's business. Princes and priests can never resist imposing restrictions on the pursuit of self-interest, division of labor, and freedom of trade. Successful pursuits mean a challenge to authority. Let people take the jobs they want and they'll seek other liberties. As for trade, nab it.

A restriction is hardly a restriction unless coercion is involved. To go back to our exemplary Cro-Magnons, a coercive trade is when I get the spear points, the mammoth meat, the cave painting, *and* the cave. What you get is killed.

Coercion destroys the mutually beneficial nature of trade, which destroys the trading, which destroys the division of labor, which destroys our self-interest. Restrain trade, however modestly, and you've made a hop and a skip toward a Maoist Great Leap Forward. Restrain either of the other economic prerogatives and the result is the same. Restrain all three and you're Mao himself.

## Adam Smith's Less Simple Principles

It is clear from Adam Smith's other writings that he was a moral advocate of freedom. But the arguments for freedom in *The Wealth of Nations* are almost uncomfortably pragmatic. Smith opposed most economic constraints: tariffs, bounties, quotas, price controls, workers in league to raise wages, employers conniving to fix pay, monopolies, cartels, royal charters, guilds, apprenticeships, indentures, and of course slavery. Smith even opposed licensing doctors, believing that licenses were more likely to legitimize quacks than the marketplace was. But Smith favored many restraints on persons, lest brute force become the coin of a lawless realm.

In words more sad and honest than we're used to hearing from an economist, Smith declared, "The peace and order of society is more important than even the relief of the miserable."

Without economic freedom the number of the miserable increases, requiring further constraints to keep the peace among them, with a consequent greater loss of freedom.

Smith was also aware that economic freedom has its discontents. He was particularly worried about the results of excess in the division of labor: "The man whose whole life is spent in performing a few simple operations... generally becomes as stupid and ignorant as it is possible for a human creature to become." We've seen this in countless politicians as they hand-shake and rote-speak their way through campaigns. But it's worth it. Productivity of every kind can be increased by specialization. And the specialization of politics at least keeps politicians from running businesses where their stupidity and ignorance could do even greater harm to economic growth.

## Adam Smith's More Complicated Principles

Smith's logical demonstration of how productivity is increased through self-interest, division of labor, and trade disproved the thesis (still dearly held by leftists and everyone's little brother) that bettering the condition of one person necessarily worsens the condition of another. Wealth is not a pizza. If I have too many slices, you don't have to eat the Domino's box.

By proving that there was no fixed amount of wealth in a nation, Smith also proved that a nation cannot be said to have a certain horde of treasure. Wealth must be measured by the volume of trades in goods and services — what goes on in the castle's kitchens and stables, not what's locked in strongboxes in the castle's tower. Smith specifies this measurement in the first sentence of his introduction to *The Wealth of Nations*. "The annual labour of every nation is the fund which originally supplies it with all the necessaries and conveniences of life which it annually consumes." Smith thereby, in a stroke, created the concept of gross domestic product. Without GDP modern economists would be left with nothing much to say, standing around mute in ugly neckties, waiting for MSNBC to ask them to be silent on the air.

If wealth is all ebb and flow, then so is its measure, money. Money has no intrinsic value. Any baby who's eaten a nickel could tell you so. And those of us old enough to have heard about the Weimar Republic and to have lived through the Carter administration are not pained by the information. But eighteenth-century money was still mostly made of precious metals. Smith's observations on money must have been slightly disheartening to his readers, although they had the example of bling-deluged but impoverished Spain to confirm what he said.

Gold is, well, worth its weight in gold, certainly, but not so certainly worth anything else. It was almost as though Smith, having proved that we can all have more money, then proved that money doesn't buy happiness. And it doesn't. It rents it.

## Adam Smith's Principles: Their Principal Effect

*The Wealth of Nations* was published, with neat coincidence, in the very year that history's greatest capitalist nation declared its independence. And to the educated people of Great Britain the notion of the United States of America was more unreasonable, counterintuitive, and, as it were, outlandish than any of Adam Smith's ideas. *Wealth* was not light reading, even by the weightier standards of eighteenth-century readers. But it was a succès d'estime and something of an actual success. The first edition sold out in six months, shocking its publisher. Other than this, there is no evidence of Smith's work shocking his contemporaries.

For instance, Smith's suggestion of the economic primacy of self-interest didn't appall anyone. That self-interest makes the world go round has been tacitly acknowledged since the world began going round — a little secret everyone knows.

And the worrisome thought that money is imaginary had been worried through by Smith's good friend David Hume a quarter of a century earlier. Indeed the fictitious quality of money had been well understood since classical times. In the two hundred years between the reigns of the emperors Nero and Gallienus, imperial fictions reduced the silver content of Roman coinage from 100 percent to none.

But, though its contents didn't make people gasp, something about *The Wealth of Nations* was grit in the gears of Enlightenment thinking. And that something is still there, grinding on our minds. I could feel it myself when the subject of self-interest came up.

None of us, in fact, take the axioms of Adam Smith as givens — not unless what's given to us are vast profits, enormous salaries, and huge year-end bonuses resulting from unfettered markets, low labor costs, increased productivity, and current Federal Reserve policy. Like the AFL-CIO, France, and various angry and addled street protestors, we quarrel with Adam Smith. If this is to be an intelligent squabble we need to examine Smith's side of the argument in full. *The Wealth of Nations* is — as my generation used to say when my generation was relevant — relevant."

*The author acknowledges material from both Sukhrit Sablok and Tarot @ www.helium.com for this particular chapter.*

# CHAPTER 10

# HAMILTON AND THE US FINANCIAL REVOLUTION (1789–1795)

## ALEXANDER HAMILTON AND THE BEGINNINGS OF THE AMERICAN FINANCIAL SYSTEM

American memory credits Alexander Hamilton mostly with bringing order and respectability to the finances of the new federal government during his tenure as the nation's first secretary of the treasury from 1789 to 1795. For that single accomplishment, his portrait appears on the face of the ten-dollar bill. The other side of that Federal Reserve note has an engraving of the Treasury Department building in Washington, D.C., with an unrecognizable statue of Hamilton on its front steps. When Robert Rubin retired as treasury secretary in 1999, President Clinton remarked from those same steps that Rubin had been the greatest occupant of the office since Alexander Hamilton. In truth, Hamilton as treasury secretary did much more than stabilize the finances of the government. When he took up his duties in 1789, the United States had none of the elements of a modern financial system. When he left office in 1795, it had all of them. Hamilton planned and executed what economic and financial historians later would call a "financial revolution."

It is a term they use to describe the creation, during a relatively brief period of history, of a modern financial system. Why should that interest us? One reason is that in today's world of hundreds of independent nations, modern economists are finding persuasive evidence that countries with stronger financial systems tend to perform better and grow faster than those with weaker systems. We economic historians agree, but see the modern findings as hardly novel. We regard financial revolutions as historically important for two reasons.

First, financial revolutions are rare events in history. Second, when they do occur, the economies of the affected countries tend thereafter to do uncommonly well compared to other countries. The United States is just one example. Here are a few others.

During the Middle Ages and the Renaissance, Italian city-states were Europe's financial innovators, and their economies became the richest on earth. Among other things, the early Italians invented modern banking. The word "bank" derives from the Italian "banco," the small table or bench on which the banker kept his accounts of deposits and loans. In early modern Europe, the tiny Dutch Republic had a financial revolution. The ability of the Dutch to borrow from their own people and others helped the republic to secured its independence from Spain, a much larger country. That and other financial innovations then led the Dutch economy into its Golden Age in the mid-seventeenth century, characterized by historian Simon Schama as "the embarrassment of riches."

It was hardly an accident that publicly traded companies, another product of the Dutch financial revolution, were the first to explore and colonize in the 1610s and 1620s what later became New York. Envious of Dutch economic and political success, England in its Glorious Revolution of 1688, invited the Dutch leader, William of Orange, to become King William III of England. William brought state-of-the-art Dutch financial practices with him. England added to them, notably by founding the Bank of England, and in the next decades had its own financial revolution. Subsequently, it experienced the first industrial revolution, became the workshop of the world in the nineteenth century, and established a great empire upon which the sun never set.

The French under John Law tried to have a financial revolution to match Britain's. But it fell apart in the 1720 collapse of Law's Mississippi Bubble, and France lagged behind Britain, financially and economically, for more than a century.

Not all attempts to have a financial revolution succeed. That is why the successful cases such as the United States are as noteworthy as they are rare.

## HAMILTON AND THE LESSONS OF FINANCIAL HISTORY

Hamilton knew this financial history, and absorbed the lessons it taught about the relationship of modern financial systems to national power and economic prosperity. Months before the Yorktown campaign in 1781, while serving as General Washington's aide-de-camp,

Hamilton wrote a letter of advice to Robert Morris, who had just become the US superintendent of finance. "'Tis by introducing order into our finances—by restoring public credit—not by gaining battles," Hamilton wrote, "that we are finally to gain our object."

Banks, he went on (at a time when America had no banks), were *the happiest engines that ever were invented for advancing trade. Venice, Genoa, Hamburg, Holland, and England are examples of their utility. They owe their riches, commerce and the figure they have made . . . to this source. Great Britain is indebted for the immense efforts she has been able to make in so many illustrious and successful wars essentially to that vast fabric of credit raised on this foundation. 'Tis by this alone she now menaces our independence.*

At the time, the War of Independence had dragged on for six long years. Congress had no power to tax; it could only requisition money from the states, which often did not comply. Money borrowed could not be repaid, making further borrowing problematic to impossible. Continental paper currency had become worthless, and the soldiers in the Continental Army were poorly supplied and ill equipped.

Hamilton saw that the way out of the mess required financial reform, which he reasoned would only be possible with fundamental political reform, that is, a new constitution. Pending that, he recommended several financial reforms to Morris and other national leaders. They included sound public finances (tax revenues to pay public expenses including the army, as well as interest on old public debts, which would make it possible to borrow more), a stable currency, a banking system, a central bank he already called the "Bank of the United States," securities markets, and corporations. The financial reforms Hamilton recommended to Morris and others in 1780 and 1781 happened to embody the key components of all modern financial systems. At the time only the English and the Dutch had them. The Americans, Hamilton deduced, needed to institute them if they wanted to secure and maintain their independence, and if they wanted to have a strong government and a prosperous, growing economy. Nearly a decade later, in 1789, the fundamental political reform—the adoption of the Constitution—had been accomplished. Indeed, Hamilton had been one of its spearheads in proposing the Philadelphia convention, serving as a New York delegate to it, and then explaining and defending it as principal author of the *Federalist Papers*. The Constitution's supporters began to call themselves Federalists. Soon they would form a political party of that name, with Hamilton as one of its leaders.

Although the United States had a new constitution in 1789, almost nothing had been done in the area of financial reform. What Hamilton and the Federalists accomplished over the next five years can perhaps best be grasped by comparing the status of each key component of a modern financial system in 1789, when Hamilton took office, and in 1795, when he left office.

### *Public Finance and Debt Management.*

When the First Congress convened in the spring of 1789, the United States government was essentially bankrupt. It had large debts on which interest had not been paid for years and no revenues to pay them. Congress then implemented a power conferred by the Constitution by enacting modest duties on imports to the United States and tonnage taxes on the ships entering US ports. That was in July 1789, even before Congress created the Treasury Department, which would have to collect these taxes. In September, when Congress did create the Treasury Department, President Washington named Hamilton to head it. Since the Treasury was empty, Hamilton immediately arranged loans from two of the country's three banks to pay government expenses. Anticipating tax revenues, Congress requested Hamilton to prepare a plan to pay the country's debt obligations. Hamilton presented his plan in January 1790. After much debate, and side deals that moved the national capital from New York to Philadelphia and then to the Potomac, Congress adopted Hamilton's plan in the summer of 1790. Fast forward to 1795. In that year, federal revenues were $6.1 million.

172

That amount was more than sufficient to pay interest of $3.2 million on a total national debt of $80 million. Hamilton had re-structured most of the country's domestic debts of nearly $70 million into three new securities issues that first appeared late in 1790. This is the origin of the Treasury bond market, which today is the largest in the world of any single issuer.

Foreign debts of some $12 million, mostly resulting from France's loans to the United States during the War of Independence, were separately serviced in Europe with new loans Hamilton arranged with Dutch bankers. The public credit of the United States was firmly established.

*Money.* In 1789, there was no US. dollar. A variety of state-issued paper currencies not convertible to hard money (except at discounted market prices) and foreign coins comprised the US money stock. Some of the paper currencies were denominated in dollars, and others in pounds of varying values in relation to one another. The US dollar came into being in 1791, when Congress adopted the recommendations of Hamilton's Mint Report submitted that year. The report

defined the dollar in terms of weights of both gold and silver, as was usually the case among the leading nations of Europe. Fast forward to 1795. The new dollar had become the unit of account for the United States. The US Mint was beginning to make silver and gold coins denominated in dollars. Upon this "hard" monetary base, new banking institutions erected a much larger super-structure of credit, with bank notes and deposits made convertible into the monetary base.

## A Banking System and a Central Bank

In 1789, there was no banking system. There were three banks, one each in Philadelphia (opened in 1782), New York (1784), and Boston (1784). They were local operations. Fast forward to 1795. There were twenty state-chartered banking corporations, plus a federally chartered Bank of the United States (bus) with its home office in Philadelphia, then the seat of the federal government, and four branches in New York, Boston, Baltimore, and Charleston. On Hamilton's recommendation, Congress created the bus in 1791. The advent of the bus stimulated the states into chartering more banks. A decade later, the bus had four more branches (in Washington, D.C., Norfolk, Savannah, and New Orleans), and the states had chartered fifty-one more banks. Thus by 1805, Americans could borrow from eighty banks, including the bus branches.

## Securities Markets

In 1789, there were no securities markets to speak of, although transactions in deeply discounted US and state securities sometimes took place. Some of these transactions were based on speculation that the new federal government might finally decide to service the country's debts. Fast forward to 1795. By then, New York, Boston, and Philadelphia hosted active securities markets with regular price quotations in newspapers.

These markets traded the three federal debt issues Hamilton had introduced late in 1790 to fund old US debts. Some $63 million (par value) of these domestic securities were outstanding. Also regularly traded and quoted were equity shares of the bus, capitalized at ten million dollars. Local securities—stocks of state banks, insurance companies, and transportation enterprises, and some state government securities—rounded out the lists. Philadelphia and New York boasted stock exchanges, created in 1790 and 1792 to handle the mushrooming trade in securities. These were brokers' clubs meeting in coffee houses. In New York's case, the exchange club established by the famous Buttonwood Agreement of 1792 did grow into *the* New York Stock Exchange, since a number of the signers in 1792 were also charter members of the modern stock exchange with formal rules and regulations established a quarter century later.

*Corporations*

In 1789, there were few corporations of any kind in the United States. In the entire colonial era, only seven business corporations had been chartered. During the 1780s, the states together chartered an average of fewer than three per year. Fast forward to 1795. By then, there were many more corporations. The pace of corporate chartering picked up noticeably in 1791, after Hamilton's bus was founded as the largest of all US corporations. States issued nine new charters that year. In 1792, there were thirty-one new charters.

175

Thus, more business corporations were created in the two years 1791-92 than had been formed in all previous years of American history. During the decade of the 1790s, charters of business corporations averaged thirty per year, more than ten times the rate of the 1780s.4

Most were non-financial corporations, but the largest ones were banks and insurance companies. From its inception, the new financial system stimulated the expansion of corporate enterprise, which in turn created demand for loans and securities to trade. As if by magic, by 1795 the United States had in place all the key elements of a modern financial system: stable public finances and national debt management, a dollar currency convertible into hard money, a banking system, a central bank, securities markets, and a host of corporations. In 1789, it lacked every one of them. This was the Federalist financial revolution planned and led by Hamilton. Its success had many consequences, two of which were a strong federal government, with its credit established at home and in international capital markets, and a more rapidly growing economy fueled both by short- and long-term credit and by equity investment.

## Controversies over the financial revolution

Since the US financial revolution succeeded, historians have tended to assume that it was accomplished easily. That was far from the case. Anti-Federalist opposition contested almost every financial measure proposed by Hamilton and the Federalists. That opposition quickly coalesced into the Republican Party led by Thomas Jefferson and James Madison. The antics of speculators and the gyrations of securities market prices, inevitable consequences of modern financial systems, served to confirm for the Republicans that the country was going down the wrong road. They tried to drive Hamilton from office by charging him with transgressing the letter or spirit of the laws. But he was able to parry the charges, and Congressional votes vindicated the treasury secretary. The later-enshrined two-party system of US politics was thus largely a product of the financial revolution. At heart, the dispute was about America's future. Jefferson and the Republicans saw Hamilton and the Federalists to be replicating eighteenth-century Great Britain, with its monarchical centralization, its

political corruption and disenfranchisement of most people, its squalid cities and factories, its speculators and stockjobbers, its high taxes, and its imperialistic, militaristic adventurism. They preferred the future to be like the past. The United States would be a decentralized republic mainly of planters and farmers, with only a thin overlay of commerce, factories, and urban life, and with governments close to the people.

Hamilton and the Federalists, in contrast, saw some virtues in British institutions. They also had faith that the US. Republican constitution, with its dual sovereignty of state and federal governments along with its checks and balances within governments, offered adequate protections against British vices. They wanted the American future to be different from past. Their future would have a strong, efficient republican government capable of protecting the country's interests in a hostile world. It would have a diversified, growing economy with agriculture, commerce, and manufacturing, all using modern financial organization to foster the rapid use of new and improved technologies. The Federalists wanted the future to be like what the future in fact turned out to be. Not long after he became president, Jefferson appeared to recognize with some bitterness that he had lost the battle with Hamilton for America's future. In 1802, he wrote:

*When this government was first established, it was possible to have kept it going on true principles, but the contracted, English, half-lettered ideas of Hamilton, destroyed that hope in the bud. We can pay off his debt in 15 years: but we can never get rid of his financial system.*5

Ironically, a year later, in 1803, Jefferson would use Hamilton's financial system to accomplish the greatest feat of his presidency: he had the United States issue $11.25 million of fresh Treasury bonds and send them to Bonaparte's government in France in payment for the Louisiana Territory.

The Louisiana Purchase doubled the size of the country. Fifteen years earlier, before the Federalist financial revolution, such a transaction would have been inconceivable for a then-bankrupt country. Daniel Webster (1782-1852), writing in 1831, three decades after Jefferson, had a different take on Hamilton. By then the United States had an industrial sector that had grown at a rate of 5 percent a year since 1790, and was well on its way to becoming the strong state with a diversified economy that the Federalists had envisioned when Webster was a child. Said Webster," *The later-enshrined two-party system of U.S. politics was thus a product of the financial revolution.*"

*The discerning eye of Washington immediately called [Hamilton] to that post, which was far the most important in the administration of the new system. He was made Secretary of the Treasury…. He smote the rock of the national resources, and abundant streams of revenue gushed forth. He touched the dead corpse of the public credit, and it sprang upon its feet. The tabled birth of Minerva from the brain of Jove was hardly more sudden or more perfect than the financial system of the United States, as it burst forth from the conceptions of Alexander Hamilton.*

In later US history, there were attempts to get rid of elements of Hamilton's financial system. They always came back. Today, public credit, the dollar, the banking system, the central bank, the securities markets, and the corporate system, although none of them is without problems, remain the envy of the world.

And the power and economic strength of the United States in the world are unmatched. Two centuries after Hamilton's death, Americans ought to remember him for starting them on the road to that result."

*This article is dedicated to RICHARD SYLLA who is Henry Kaufman Professor of the History of Financial Institutions and Markets at the Stern School of Business, New York University. He is also a research associate of the National Bureau of Economic Research and a former editor of the Journal of Economic History. His current research focus is on the financial history of the United States in comparative contexts.*

# CHAPTER 11

## AMERICA'S FIRST FINANCIAL CRISIS: THE PANIC OF 1819

A financial panic may be defined as a period falling prices and business failures characterized by a sudden loss of public confidence in the stability of financial institutions such as banks or in the stock markets. A cardinal feature of such panics is that a bank's depositors will, out of concerns for the bank's solvency, attempt to withdraw their deposits from that bank at the same time. This action is usually referred to as a "bank run" and invariably "makes a bad situation worse" (Note 1)

In this posting we will examine the first such nationwide financial panic to have struck the young American Republic, the Panic of 1819. But, in order to understand the roots of that panic, it will be necessary to review the significant events of the first two decades of the 19th Century.

Between 1803 and 1815 England, and an on-again off-again coalition of European nations, had been at war with Napoleon Bonaparte's France (the Napoleonic Wars). As part of its strategy to weaken the French economy by disrupting its foreign trade, England had deployed its formidable navy to prevent merchant shipping into (and out of) French ports. Since America, although officially neutral, had been trading with both sides of the conflict, the loss of exports to France represented a serious (but not catastrophic) blow to the national economy (Note 2).

American President Thomas Jefferson, who favored France in his personal sentiments, retaliated with a series of trade embargoes against England between 1806 and 1808.

As a result of both the American and English actions, American exports to Europe dwindled to less than 90% of its pre-1806 volume (Note 3). By the time Jefferson lifted the embargoes near the end of his terms in office in 1808, Canada had emerged as a significant source of competition for the emerging American industrial base. By the middle of James Madison's first term in office (1809-1813) he was under intense pressure from the northeastern states to declare war on England, which would serve as an excuse to invade Canada and thus remove it as a source of economic competition. Madison succumbed to this pressure in 1812 by ordering the American army to move against Canada. The result was the American-British War of 1812 which, in turn, led to the consequences of the worst mistake (other than invading Canada) made by Madison during his 8 years in office: his decision not to renew the charter that had established the Bank of the United States.

Alexander Hamilton, the first American Secretary of the Treasury, had pressed for the establishment of an American central bank that would be modeled after the Bank of England. The leaders of the anti-Federalist movement (such as Madison), fearing a concentration of financial power on the national level, favored instead a system of state-chartered banks.

Hamilton's views (which were beneficial to the industrial northeastern states) eventually prevailed in Congress and the (First) Bank of the United States, which would serve as the repository of Federal revenues as well act as the agent for the sale and redemptions of government bonds, was issued a Congressional charter in 1791.

However, as a part of the compromises that led to its approval, this charter would expire after 20 years unless it was renewed by another act of Congress.

In 1811, Madison had vetoed the law renewing the bank's charter and federal income was redistributed among the state banks. This veto also meant that, when war was declared a year later, there was no American central bank that could readily raise money to finance the war by the selling of government bonds. Instead, the state banks (rather haphazardly) became the agents for selling Government bonds and then disbursing the funds received to pay the government's debts. Following the war, the government faced the daunting challenge of paying back the money it had borrowed to finance that war. Since tariffs and excise taxes (which had been disrupted by lack of foreign trade) were only slowly recovering from the disruption caused by the war, and since they were the only source of government revenues, it was vitally necessary for the American government to find new sources of revenue. Fortunately, there was a potential source of government income that was, literally, just lying there: land.

Thanks to the Northwest Ordinance (1789) and the Louisiana Purchase (1803), the government of the United States owned over 1 million square miles of unsettled and undeveloped land that it could sell to anyone that would be willing to develop that land into working farms and townships.

The federal government's plan was quite simple: sell the unsettled land to anyone that was willing to pay $1.25 per acre for a minimum purchase of 40 acres. The proceeds from these sales would then go to the Second Bank of the United States (Note 3) where it would then be used to pay off the government's debts. As in the case of most "simple" plans, the situation soon became quite complicated

Land speculators would purchase large tracts of land at the government's asking price of $1.25 per acre and then divide their large purchases into smaller tracts that they would then resell to settlers at up to $5.00 dollars per acre. If a settler couldn't afford the price of the land, they could easily borrow the purchase price from a state-chartered bank that happened to be owned by the speculators themselves. The new Bank of the United States, in keeping with its mission as stated in its charter, would then loan money to the speculators' new banks that would pledge the settlers' mortgages as collateral for the loans. In practicality, the Bank of the United States was loaning the speculators' purchase money back to the banks that the speculators themselves owned.

Initially, as long as the settlers were able to meet their obligations to their local banks by selling their crops, the system worked to everyone's satisfaction If the prices from their crops should drop, however, the banks' cash flow would then be insufficient to meet its obligations to its depositors, other state banks, and to the Bank of the United States. This is precisely what happened when agricultural prices began to fall in 1818 (Note 4).

As prices declined, the settlers fell behind on their obligations to the banks. The state banks were then unable to meet their own obligations regarding money owed to the Bank of the United States as well as the sudden demands by depositors wanting to withdraw their money from the now-distressed state banks. Although it would have been to the Bank of the United States' advantage to come to the support of the state banks by making emergency loans to provide sufficient funds to get the banks through their times of vulnerability, it was unable to do so because it had only been in existence for 2 years and its own solvency would have then been difficult to maintain As the banks begin to fail, not only did these failures disrupt their local economies but they cause a significant reduction in the amount of money then in circulation throughout the nation.

At the time, the United States Treasury did not directly issue money. Money, in the form of banknotes, was instead issued by private banks.

In theory, a state bank could not issue its own banknotes unless those notes were "backed up" by government bonds in the banks possession or by gold and silver that the bank had stored in its vaults. Since there was practically no government supervision of banks that were issuing their own banknotes, there was no incentive for the banks to follow those requirements. Instead, most banks simply printed money when the need arose.

As individual banks began to fail their banknotes, which were supposedly secured by the assets of the banks themselves, became worthless because no one would accept a promise to pay made by a bank that was no longer in existence. As the supply of circulating money rapidly fell, it became harder for businesses to pay for both the raw materials used to manufacture other goods and the labor of workers that would produce those goods in exchange for wages. The Panic of 1819 thus directly led to the cycle of business failures followed by unemployment that persisted for two years and would eventually become known as the Depression of 1819–1821.

In conclusion, the Panic of 1819 was not caused by either a specific internal or external action but was rather the result of a chain of events. The inability of Congress to override Madison's veto of its earlier legislation extending the charter of the Bank of the United States was a critical factor in that Panic because the ability of the Bank of the United States to intervene by supporting the state banks in their earliest days of crisis was severely limited by the fact that it had not been able to establish sufficient capital to finance such an intervention.

Notes

1. During a bank run, a bank will not have enough cash on hand to meet the demands of its depositors and will be force to close while it attempts to raise money to by either selling its portfolio (at a discounted price) of loans to another bank or by "calling in" (demanding payment) on those                                                                loans.

2. Carl Benn, "The War of 1812," (New York: Osprey, 2002).

3. Madison, after seeing the financial chaos caused by the lack of a central bank, reversed his position in 1816 and signed into law the bill authorizing the charter of the Bank of the United States, which is usually referred to as the Second Bank of the United States.

4. The exact sequence of events is given in Murray Rothbard, "The Panic of 1819: Reactions and Policies," (Auburn, AL: Ludwig von Mises Institute, 2002).

*This chapter exposition is credited to an article written by Robert W. Mcdonald in* www.helium.com

# CHAPTER 12

## THE US FINANCIAL PANIC OF 1837

The **Panic of 1837** was an economic depression, one of the sharpest financial crises in the history of the United States. The Panic was built on a speculative fever. The bubble burst on May 10, 1837 in New York City, when every bank stopped payment in specie (gold and silver coinage). The Panic was followed by a six-year depression, with the failure of banks and record unemployment levels.

## 1 Causes

Causes include the economic policies of President Andrew Jackson, including the Specie Circular and the withdrawal of government funds from the Second Bank of the United States. Martin van Buren, President during 1837 was blamed for the Panic. His refusal to involve the government in the economy contributed to the damages and duration of the Panic.

### 1.1 The banking system

Jackson began his first administration by withdrawing all federal deposits from the Bank of the United States, whose charter was allowed to lapse in 1836, based on a Jackson veto. The Federal funds were distributed to local and state banks, fuelling the boom.

## 1.2 Inflationary boom of the 1830s

The boom of the early 1830s was led by the construction of new canals and schemes that would eventually provide the first network of railroads. The Federal government encouraged the speculative fever by selling millions of acres of public lands in western states like Michigan and Missouri, mostly to speculators, who resold and bought, in hopes of assembling well-located parcels that would quickly increase in real value as well as paper value, once the turnpikes and canals and the promised railroads brought settlers and traffic.

The U.S. Treasury was accumulating a budget surplus, which members of Congress voted to distribute in the spring of 1837, passing the funds to their home districts, where the windfall was quickly invested-- in canals, turnpikes and railroad companies.

## 1.3 A failure of confidence in banknotes

Meanwhile the compromise tariff bill enacted in 1833 (after South Carolina's portentous threat of secession) was reducing the Federal government's income, which depended heavily on excise taxes, while at the same time Andrew Jackson's administration worked to pay off the national debt, in 1835.

The Jackson Administration, like many private individuals, preferred the secure value of gold and silver (payments in specie 'by coin') to payment in notes from the multitude of all but unregulated local banks. Jackson and his Secretary of the Treasury, Levi WoodburyLevi Woodbury ( December 22, 1789 September 4, 1851) was the first justice of the Supreme Court of the United States to have attended law school. Woodbury was born in Francestown, New Hampshire. He graduated from Dartmouth College in 1809, briefly attendee of New Hampshire, issued the Specie Circular, commanding that as of August 15, 1836, the U.S. Treasury cease to accept banknotes as payment for public lands. It was a vote of 'no confidence' in paper money at the highest level.

Many state banks and the 'wildcat' local banks did not have specie to back their paper, when a bank run occurred; instead of the expected flood of gold and silver coming to the national treasury, land sales dropped to a quarter of the previous year's level, companies started paying their workers in scrip, i.o.u's began to circulate, specie payments defaulted. The Western demand for coin was quickly transferred to New York City, linked now to the west through the Erie Canal. A full-fledged financial crisis greeted Martin van Buren's inauguration in March 1837. During the first three weeks of April, two hundred and fifty business houses failed in New York. On May 10, 1837, every bank in New York suspended payment in specie.

## 2. Effects and Aftermath

Within two months the failures in New York alone aggregated nearly $100,000,000. "Out of eight hundred and fifty banks in the United States, three hundred and forty-three closed entirely, sixty-two failed partially, and the system of State banks received a shock from which it never fully recovered."[1]

A central banking cushion of any sort might have prevented some local failures. A few large local banks, like the Suffolk Bank of Boston, acted like central banks, lending reserves to other banks, and alleviated the effects of the Panic of 1837 in New England. Though van Buren did not engender the Panic of 1837, he was harshly judged (and failed to be re-elected) because he was ideologically committed to keeping the government out of banking regulation, a resolve that many economic historians feel extended the effects of the Panic, which was not over until 1843. Van Buren even kept Jackson's Secretary of the Treasury, Levi Woodbury.

# CHAPTER 13

## SUMMARY OF MAJOR AND MINOR FINANCIAL PANICS

## IN 19th CENTURY US

Severe Economic Depressions Occurred Periodically. The Great Depression of the 1930s was called "great" for a reason. It followed a long series of depressions which afflicted the American economy throughout the 19th century. Crop failures, drops in cotton prices, reckless railroad speculation, and sudden plunges in the stock market all came together at various times to send the growing American economy into chaos. The effects were often brutal, with millions of Americans losing jobs, farmers being forced off their land, and railroads, banks, and other businesses going under for good.

Here are the basic facts on the major financial panics of the 19th century.

## Panic of 1819

- The first major American depression, the Panic of 1819 was rooted to some extent in economic problems reaching back to the war of 1812.

- It was triggered by a collapse in cotton prices. A contraction in credit coincided with the problems in the cotton market, and the young American economy was severely affected.
- Banks were forced to call in loans, and foreclosures of farms and bank failures resulted.
- The Panic of 1819 lasted until 1821.
- The effects were felt most in the west and south. Bitterness about the economic hardships resonated for years and led to the resentment that helped Andrew Jackson solidify his political base throughout the 1820s.

- Besides exacerbating sectional animosity, the Panic of 1819 also made many Americans realize the importance of politics and government policy in their lives.

# Panic of 1837

- The Panic of 1837 was triggered by a combination of factors including the failure of a wheat crop, a collapse in cotton prices, economic problems in Britain, rapid speculation in land, and problems resulting from the variety of currency in circulation.
- It was the second-longest American depression, with effects lasting roughly six years, until 1843.
- The panic had a devastating impact. A number of brokerage firms in New York failed, and at least one New York City bank president committed suicide. As the effect rippled across the nation, a number of state-chartered banks also failed. The nascent labor union movement was effectively stopped, as the price of labor plummeted.
- The depression caused the collapse of real estate prices. The price of food also collapsed, which was ruinous to farmers and planters who couldn't get a decent price for their crops. People who lived through the depression following 1837 told stories that would be echoed a century later during The Great Depression.

- The aftermath of the panic of 1837 led to Martin Van Buren's failure to secure a second term in the election of 1840. Many blamed the economic hardships on the policies of Andrew Jackson, and Van Buren, who had been Jackson's vice president, paid the political price.

## Panic of 1857

- The Panic of 1857 was triggered by the failure of the Ohio Life Insurance and Trust Company, which actually did much of its business as a bank headquartered in New York City. Reckless speculation in railroads led the company into trouble, and the company's collapse led to a literal panic in the financial district, as crowds of frantic investors clogged the streets around Wall Street.
- Stock prices plummeted, and more than 900 mercantile firms in New York had to cease operation. By the end of the year the American economy was a shambles.
- One victim of the Panic of 1857 was a future Civil War hero and US president, Ulysses S. Grant, who was bankrupted and had to pawn his gold watch to buy Christmas presents.
- Recovery from the depression began in early 1859.

## Panic of 1873

- The investment firm of Jay Cooke and Company went bankrupt in September 1873 as a result of rampant speculation in railroads. The stock market dropped sharply and caused numerous businesses to fail.
- The depression caused approximately three million Americans to lose their jobs.
- The collapse in food prices impacted America's farm economy, causing great poverty in rural America.
- The depression lasted for five years, until 1878.

- The Panic of 1873 led to a populist movement that saw the creation of the Greenback Party.

## Panic of 1893

- The depression set off by the Panic of 1893 was the greatest depression America had known, and was only surpassed by the Great Depression of the 1930s.
- In early May 1893 the New York stock market dropped sharply, and in late June panic selling caused the stock market to crash.
- A severe credit crisis resulted, and more than 16,000 businesses had failed by the end of 1893. Included in the failed businesses were 156 railroads and nearly 500 banks.
- Unemployment spread until one in six American men lost their jobs.
- The depression inspired "Coxey's Army," a march on Washington of unemployed men. The protesters demanded that the government provide public works jobs. Their leader, Jacob Coxey, was imprisoned for 20 days.
- The depression caused by the Panic of 1893 lasted for about four years, ending in 1897.

*This chapter exposition is credited to the works of Robert McNamara in his discussions on 19th century panics as expressed in about.com*

# CHAPTER 14

## AMERICAN CIVIL WAR AS A BASIS FOR 1893 SILVER PANIC

Following the American Civil War, Silver was discovered in huge quantity in the Comstock Lode near Virginia City, Nevada. Supporters of freely minted silver proposed both silver and gold be used as the standards to support the United States monetary reserves. Silver was proposed to be introduced at $1 per troy ounce. The result of this policy would have been a considerable increase in the money supply and resultant inflation. Inflation was not regarded with the near-universal disdain in which it is held today. Free Silver supporters, whose ranks were swelled by many agrarian, populist, and radical organizations, favored an inflationary monetary policy on the grounds that it enabled debtors (often farmers, laborers, and industrial workers) to pay their debts off with cheaper, more readily-available dollars. Those who would have suffered under this policy were the wealthy creditors such as banks, leaseholders, and landlords, who under this theory could well afford any loss this caused them.

In the view of his party, to keep the country operating on the gold standard, Cleveland ordered the Treasury Department to sell U.S. Government bonds to New York City bankers in exchange for gold bullion. This was one of the most unpopular things Cleveland ever did, because many Americans became alarmed over the dependence of the government on a syndicate of Wall Street bankers. Panic ensued and the situation was ripe for a silver panic---- the 1893 Silver Panic lasted for four long years and created economic havoc in the United States.

## CHAPTER 15

## THE 1893 SILVER PANIC IN THE UNITED STATES:

## A DETAILED STUDY

The Panic of 1893 was perhaps the hardest depression in American history, in terms of its total impact. Thousands of banks closed, millions went out of work, and the westward expansion that had defined the post-Civil War era vanished for nearly 25 years. It is a wanton tale of greed, overregulation, and ignorance. But first, a little economics 101.

For whatever reason as nature saw fit, silver and gold were selected to be the primary metals by which our monetary standard in America and abroad is governed. Due to various market rules regarding supply and demand, gold had more or less been 15 times as valuable as silver in terms of trading and the market. Recognizing this ratio, then-Secretary of the Treasury Alexander Hamilton declared this the fixed ratio for dealing with the metals in the federal government in 1792.

There is a little known law, Gresham's Law, which states that when two monies are set at fixed ratios, then the bad money (money that is overvalued) will drive out the good money (money that is undervalued) from the market. In this case, gold was actually trading at a rate closer to 15½ to 1. Thus on the bullion market a piece of gold could get you 15½ pieces of silver. Soon silver flew freely into the mint (since an investor got a better deal from the government for it) and became coined more, while gold vanished into hiding or to overseas market. In time, a de facto silver standard existed in the United States.

To remedy this, in 1834 Congress changed the ratio to 16 to 1. Unfortunately, the real ratio had not changed much in that time, and now gold become overvalued and soon gold was being traded at high volume. To make matters worse, gold was much more expensive in general than silver, and thus only richer people could afford to speculate on the bullion market and deal with the treasury.

Now that we understand a bit more about the commodities market and the general flow of currency, let's resume our history lesson. In 1870, shortly following the Civil War, a political party was formed whose sole purpose was to artificially inflate the U.S. economy. During the Civil War, the Union had printed paper money called "greenbacks", which they had traded much like the war bonds of today in order to fund the Army. After the war, the Greenback Party was formed for the sole purpose of expanding this paper money supply into its own flexible market.

They claimed (partially correctly) that the current hard money standard based on silver and gold mainly benefited the rich, but that a flexible supply could be manipulated by the government to help working people, particularly farmers in the West and South.

The Party fought hard to create the supply, but instead was met with the Specie Resumption Act of 1875, which offered a gold redemption for the currently issued greenbacks, and a limit of $100,000,000 in greenbacks to be kept in circulation, backed by gold.

The next step towards disaster was the free silver movement that dominated the early 1880s. Since gold was overvalued, and silver undervalued, the demand for silver had dropped significantly, and with it, its market price. This was actually a modified plan of the inflationist's before, to reduce the impact of hard money by making the government a trading tool for silver, which was much cheaper than gold. With the Blaid-Allison Act of 1878, the government agreed to buy $2 million worth of silver every month, and to coin it at a rate of 16 to 1, the lawful ratio. This foolhardy measure (silver was currently trading at the ludicrous rate of 18¼ to 1) was vetoed by then-President Rutherford B. Hayes, but overridden by Congress. Soon, silver speculators and mine owners alike were taking silver to the government, and then returning with more gold than they would be paid on the real market. In turn, they would use the gold to acquire even more mines and cover the costs of production.

Silver miners were essentially being subsidized by the government for their work, when the free market would've driven most of them out of business due to lack of demand. This subsidization was only worsened by the Sherman Silver Purchase Act of 1890, which legislated that the Treasury buy 4.5 million ounces of silver per month – essentially the entire output of silver mines in America.

At the same time that America was moving towards this hard silver standard at the unreasonable rate of 16 to 1, nearly every other world economy had *dropped the silver standard altogether.* Holland, France, Denmark, Austria-Hungary, England, Italy, Greece, and Russia had all gone to the gold standard, leaving America alone as the single silver-backed economy in the major powers of the world. And now, for some more economics 101.

The overabundance of silver in the coin supply made its market value continue to decline (although silver mine owners still made a healthy profit through the government.) From 1878 to 1895 a 371¼ grain silver dollar had plummeted nearly 40% in value. What made matters worse was that many people who had entered into contracts with promises to be repaid in coin, were being paid back in silver, which had lost considerable value since the contract had been entered into. Even worse, since silver had become such an easy sell to the government, and the government only had gold to pay out, gold reserves had become seriously depleted within the Treasury.

This had the added effect of limiting production in the country, due to people's reluctance to depend on the gold that may or may not be in the bank when payment was due. Back to the history.

In response, many foreign investors began abandoning the American securities market, and in fact, many Americans began spending their capital in Latin America and Canada, predicting the collapse of the U.S. economy in a self-fulfilling prophecy. The cycle of silver to gold to more silver had increased circulation of paper money and silver in the country by nearly 75% in the past 20 years, causing the inflation that the Greenback Party had so desired. This inflation caused more investors in the open market, and loan rates dropped considerably to accommodate these new borrowers. Call margins grew outrageously, and soon loans had exceeded the physical reserves of the banks. All of the classic warning signs of a panic were there; simply nothing was done to solve it.

Finally in January 1893, the rising prices of industry began to recede, part of the cyclical nature of the economy and showing no particular biases or evidences. Banks in their nature are conservative beasts; they began calling in their formerly "easy money" loans as quickly as they had handed them out. The credit industry dropped nearly 20% in the two months following. Finally, on February 20, 1893, the Reading Railroad declared bankruptcy on $18 million worth of debt and only $100,000 of accounts receivable.

When President Benjamin Harrison left office on March 4, many merchants were already refusing to accept the highly inflated silver as payment, and many factories were going on strike, because their employers chose to pay them in silver certificates.

On May 3, 1893, a huge brawl ensued on the New York Stock Exchange floor, as banks called in loans and panicked business owners rushed to sell off their flailing companies before their stocks went completely belly up. The following day, National Cordage Trust provided a harrowing example of the folly of the entire silver standard as it stood:

*In the Cordage Trust circle of the New York Stock Exchange, hats were being smashed, coats torn, cravats ruined. Here was an agony that meant financial life or death to many. Cordage common had gone off 18 points. The preferred had lost 22. Suddenly howls went up from the floor. Those who could distinguish the words, heard the ominous cry: "Nineteen for Cordage!"*

*The shares, a few moments later, went down to $12.*

Within weeks, hundreds of companies had gone out of businesses and locked up their gates. By July of 1893, 3400 companies had gone bust, with over $169,000,000 lost in the economy.

That same month, Grover Cleveland ordered a special session of Congress to repeal the Sherman Purchase Act and end the fixed trading that had caused so much disaster in America.

Finally on August 28, the Sherman Act was repealed. Unfortunately, it would take another 4 years for the Panic's effect to lessen, and by then, thousands of people across America had literally starved to death, waiting on checks that they simply couldn't cash.

The **Panic of 1893** was a serious economic depression in the United States that began in 1893. This panic is sometimes considered a part of the Long Depression which began with the Panic of 1873,[1] and like that of earlier crashes, was caused by railroad overbuilding and shaky railroad financing which set off a series of bank failures. Compounding market overbuilding and a railroad bubble was a run on the gold supply and a policy of using both gold and silver metals as a peg for the US Dollar value. The severity was great in all industrial cities and mill towns. Farm distress was great because of the falling prices for export crops such as wheat and cotton. Coxey's Army was a highly publicized march of unemployed laborers from Ohio and Pennsylvania to Washington to demand relief. A severe wave of strikes took place in 1894, most notably the Midwestern bituminous coal strike of the spring, which led to violence in Ohio. Even more serious was the Pullman Strike, which shut down much of the nation's transportation system in July, 1894.

The Sherman Silver Purchase Act of 1890, perhaps along with the protectionist McKinley Tariff of 1890, have been partially blamed for the panic. Passed in response to a large overproduction of silver by western mines, the Sherman Act required the U.S. Treasury to purchase silver using notes backed by either silver or gold. Politically, the Democrats and President Cleveland were blamed for the depression. The Democrats and Populists lost heavily in the 1894 elections, which marked the largest Republican gains in history.

Many of the western silver mines closed, and a large number were never re-opened. A significant number of western mountain narrow-gauge railroads, which had been built to serve the mines, also went out of business. The Denver and Rio Grande Railroad stopped its ambitious plan, then under way, to convert its system from narrow-gauge to standard-gauge.

The depression was a major issue in the debates over Bimetallism. The Republicans blamed the Democrats and scored a landslide victory in the 1894 state and Congressional elections. The Populists lost most of their strength and had to support the Democrats in 1896. The presidential election of 1896 was fought on economic issues and was marked by a decisive victory of the pro-gold, high-tariff Republicans led by William McKinley over pro-silver William Jennings Bryan.

Many people abandoned their homes and came west. The growing railway towns in the west of Seattle, Portland, Salt Lake City, Denver, San Francisco and Los Angeles took in the populations, as did many smaller centers.

The U.S. economy finally began to recover in 1896. After the election of Republican McKinley, confidence was restored with the Klondike gold rush and the economy began 10 years of rapid growth, until the Panic of 1907.

References

1. ^ Fels, Rendigs (1949). "The Long-Wave Depression, 1873-97". *The Review of Economics and Statistics* 31: 69. doi:10.2307/1927196. http://www.jstor.org/pss/1927196.
2. ^ Steel magnate Andrew Carnegie, for example, made millions selling steel rails.
3. ^ James L. Holton, *The Reading Railroad: History of a Coal Age Empire*, Vol. I: The Nineteenth Century, pp. 323-325, citing Vincent Corasso, *The Morgans*.
4. ^ The History Box, The Panic of 1893 – Financial World; accessed 2009.04.08.
5. ^ The Encyclopedia of Arkansas History and Culture, The Panic of 1893; accessed 2009.04.08.
6. ^ *a* *b* Whitten, David O.. "EH.Net Encyclopedia: Depression of 1893". eh.net. http://eh.net/encyclopedia/article/whitten.panic.1893. Retrieved 2009-04-20.

7. ^ Hoffman, Charles. The Depression of the Nineties: An Economic History. Westport, CT: Greenwood Publishing, 1970. Page 109.

External references

**Primary sources**

- *Appleton's Annual Cyclopedia and Register of Important Events for the Year* (annual 1893–1897).
- Baum, Lyman Frank and W. W. Denslow. *The Wonderful Wizard of Oz* (1900).
- Brice, Lloyd Stephens, and James J. Wait. "The Railway Problem." *North American Review* 164 (March 1897): 327–48. online at MOA Cornell.
- Cleveland, Frederick A. "The Final Report of the Monetary Commission." *Annals of the American Academy of Political and Social Science* 13 (January 1899): 31–56 (JSTOR).
- Closson, Carlos C. Jr. "The Unemployed in American Cities." *Quarterly Journal of Economics*, vol. 8, no. 2 (January 1894) 168–217 (JSTOR).
- Closson, Carlos C. Jr. "The Unemployed in American Cities," *Quarterly Journal of Economics,* vol. 8, no. 4 (July 1894): 443–477 (JSTOR).
- Fisher, Willard. "'Coin' and His Critics." *Quarterly Journal of Economics* 10 (January 1896): 187–208 (JSTOR).
- Harvey, William H. *Coin's Financial School* (1894), 1963 (Introduction by Richard Hofstadter).

- Noyes, Alexander Dana. "The Banks and the Panic." *Political Science Quarterly* 9 (March 1894): 12–28 (JSTOR).
- Shaw, Albert. "Relief for the Unemployed in American Cities." *Review of Reviews* 9 (January and February 1894): 29–37, 179–91.
- Stevens, Albert Clark. "An Analysis of the Phenomena of the Panic in the United States in 1893." *Quarterly Journal of Economics* 8 (January 1894): 117–48 (JSTOR).

## Secondary sources

- Barnes, James A. *John G. Carlisle: Financial Statesman* (1931).
- Barnes, James A. (1947). "Myths of the Bryan Campaign". *Mississippi Valley Historical Review* **34**: 383–394. doi:10.2307/1898096.
- Destler, Chester McArthur. *American Radicalism, 1865–1901* (1966).
- Dewey, Davis Rich. *Financial History of the United States* (1903).
- Dighe, Ranjit S. ed. *The Historian's Wizard of Oz: Reading L. Frank Baum's Classic as a Political and Monetary Allegory* (2002).
- Dorfman, Joseph Harry. *The Economic Mind in American Civilization.* (1949). vol 3.
- Faulkner, Harold Underwood. *Politics, Reform, and Expansion, 1890–1900.* (1959).

- Feder, Leah Hanna. *Unemployment Relief in Periods of Depression ... 1857–1920* (1926).
- Friedman, Milton, and Anna Jacobson Schwartz. *A Monetary History of the United States, 1867–1960* (1963).
- Holton, James L. *The Reading Railroad: History of a Coal Age Empire*, Vol. I: The Nineteenth Century. Garrigues House, Publishers, Laury's Station, Pennsylvania. 1989.
- Hoffmann, Charles (1956). "The Depression of the Nineties". *Journal of Economic History* **16** (2): 137–164. doi:10.2307/2114113.
- Hoffmann, Charles. *The Depression of the Nineties: An Economic History* (1970).
- Jensen, Richard. *The Winning of the Midwest: 1888–1896* (1971).
- Josephson, Matthew. *The Robber Barons* New York: Harcourt Brace Jovanovich (1990).
- Kirkland, Edward Chase. *Industry Comes of Age, 1860–1897* (1961).
- Lauck, William Jett. jays journal *The Causes of the Panic of 1893* (1907).
- Lindsey, Almont. *The Pullman Strike* 1942.
- Littlefield, Henry M. (1964). "The Wizard of Oz: Parable on Populism". *American Quarterly* **16** (1): 47–58. doi:10.2307/2710826.
- Nevins, Allan. *Grover Cleveland: A Study in Courage.* 1932, Pulitzer Prize.

- Rezneck, Samuel S. (1953). "Unemployment, Unrest, and Relief in the United States during the Depression of 1893-97". *Journal of Political Economy* **61** (4): 324-345. doi:10.2307/1826883.
- Ritter, Gretchen. *Goldbugs and Greenbacks: The Anti-Monopoly Tradition and the Politics of Finance in America* (1997)
- Ritter, Gretchen (1997). "Silver slippers and a golden cap: L. Frank Baum's The Wonderful Wizard of Oz and historical memory in American politics". *Journal of American Studies* **31** (2): 171-203. doi:10.1017/S0021875897005628.
- Rockoff, Hugh (1990). "The 'Wizard of Oz' as a Monetary Allegory". *Journal of Political Economy* **98** (4): 739-760. doi:10.2307/2937766.
- Romer, Christina (1986). "Spurious Volatility in Historical Unemployment Data". *Journal of Political Economy* **94** (1): 1-37. doi:10.1086/261361.
- Schwantes, Carlos A. *Coxey's Army: An American Odyssey* (1985).
- Shannon, Fred Albert. *The Farmer's Last Frontier: Agriculture, 1860-1897* (1945).
- Steeples, Douglas, and David O. Whitten. *Democracy in Desperation: The Depression of 1893* (1998).
- White; Gerald T. *The United States and the Problem of Recovery after 1893* 1982.
- Whitten, David. EH.NET article on the Depression of 1893

211

# CHAPTER 16

## 1907 PANIC

Ever since the "Panic of 1907," the United States and the world have been buffeted by financial storms of varying intensity. There had been earlier financial disasters, some of them far-reaching (such as "Hard Times" of the 1830s and "Black Friday" of the 1890s), but virtually everyone who thought about it was able to pinpoint the cause of such things, and understand them. "Hard Times," for example, were a direct result of Andrew Jackson's trade embargo, while the depression of the 1870s was due to a constriction of the money supply in an effort to restore the "faith and credit" of the United States following the Civil War.

The Panic of 1907 was different, however. Briefly, the president of a small New York Bank, the Knickerbocker Bank and Trust, had gotten his bank into financial trouble by speculating in copper shares (that is, shares in copper mining companies). Foreseeing a "run" on the bank, as it is called when depositors all start demanding their money at once, the Knickerbocker president applied to J. P. Morgan (who had a virtual monopoly on money and credit in the United States at the time) for a liquidity loan to keep his bank from closing.

As a side note, all the depositors, or even a significant number of them demanding their money is an impossible demand to meet. The money is lent out and exists only in the form of debt paper owed to the bank – remember the famous scene in "It's a Wonderful Life" when Jimmy Stewart tries to explain this to the Savings and Loan customers? nothing bank. He refused the loan, thinking to pick up the Knickerbocker's business and customers on the cheap. He also shut down clearing house privileges for the numerous small banks in and around New York City, which (as Morgan controlled the clearing houses) effectively prevented small banks from carrying out business.

The result was the Panic of 1907, which Morgan had certainly not anticipated. A worldwide recession quickly developed, and many small to mid–size banks went out of business. Morgan went into action, and started supplying money and credit on a vast scale. In some eyes even today this made him a public benefactor, but only if we forget that he caused the situation in the first place, and that his providing money and credit at a critical time also made him enormous profits. In response to the Congressional investigations that followed, the Federal Reserve System was established. The idea was to ensure that there would always be sufficient money and credit for industry, agriculture, and commerce, to regulate the commercial banks, and to break Morgan's monopoly on money and credit, a monopoly centered in New York City (this is why there are a dozen regional Federal Reserve Banks, not a single central bank).

There was also a provision to prevent the government being able to create money at will to finance its operations through borrowing rather than taxation (note that the Internal Revenue Act was passed at the same time as the Federal Reserve Act).

The Federal Reserve System, if operated in accordance with the Federal Reserve Act, would thus ensure that something like the Panic of 1907 would never again occur. Unfortunately, because of World War One, the Federal Reserve virtually stopped providing money and credit for industry, agriculture, and commerce, and became effectively (despite the original intent) the lender of first resort for the government.

In the post war world (World War One, that is), it became fixed in people's minds that "investment" meant buying and selling shares on Wall Street. The only way to provide sufficient money and credit for industry, agriculture, and commerce was to float an issue of securities on Wall Street, and wait for the money to roll in. The Federal Reserve limited its participation in the productive sector of the economy to fiddling around with reserve requirements of commercial banks, a dangerous and volatile method of implementing monetary policy Consequently, Wall Street – a "secondary market" for securities – has become in the eyes of the public and government policy makers the primary market for raising investment capital.

Unfortunately, the vast majority of activity on Wall Street (wherever an exchange may physically be located) is speculation, not investment. That is, in speculation you don't buy something with which to produce a good or a service, but make a purchase in the hope that the price of the thing you bought will increase, and you can sell it at a profit. Thus, the whole of the American economy – despite the fact that the productive sector remains relatively strong despite all the shocks it has endured – behaves as if the speculation on Wall Street were the real economy, instead of a second-hand shop for used stocks and bonds. If this remains unchanged, there will be a financial meltdown to dwarf that of October, 1929. Fortunately, however, people are starting to pay attention to a proposed reform of the financial and economic system. This proposal, developed by the Center for Economic and Social Justice, CESJ, www.cesj.org, is called "capital homesteading."

Capita l homesteading is designed to restructure the economic along productive, rather than speculative lines, and (to make certain that no one has a monopoly over money, credit, or ownership of the means of production) to ensure that as many people as possible have a significant and meaningful ownership (meaning investment, not speculation) stake in the productive capital of the country in which they live.

*This Chapter is dedicated to Michael Greaney and his path-breaking article in www.helium.com*

# CHAPTER 17

## FLORIDA REAL ESTATE BUBBLE 1926

The 1920's decade was a time of growing prosperity for Americans. Most Americans had decent jobs, a good pension plan and adequate vacation time every year. In addition, they had disposable income and were considering expanding and enhancing their lifestyle. Florida always seemed a worthwhile destination for millions of Americans, who wanted to escape the Northern winters and cold. With a developing railroad transportation system and relatively cheap land, Florida was destined to develop into a world class tourism and recreation playground.

A lot of families started taking yearly holidays in Florida and slowly but surely tourism took off. Along with more tourists and some new land investors the impact was now felt on real estate values. Slowly in the beginning but ever moving upwards, the real estate market took off.

As the 1920's decade progressed more and more wealthier individuals started buying land and homes in Florida. Credit was plentiful and one could buy a house with little or no money down. This is when even middle income Americans got into the picture and started snapping up Florida properties.

As prices started increasing, the run up in prices caught the attention of Northern US real estate speculators who now started buying lands and homes in Florida at a meteoric pace. There was so much real estate activity that the Miami Herald ( a local Miami newspaper) in 1922 became the heaviest newspaper in the world with thousands of  buy and sell real state ads. Soon all the new residents coming to Florida were either investors or real estate agents.

To make matters worse and fuel the speculative fever more, individuals like Carl Fisher of Miami beach, purchased and displayed a huge board in New York Times Square. His message in this hoarding read," Its June in Miami." As more and more investors piled on to real estate, prices doubled and quadrupled. However, as the history of bubbles always indicated speculatively high asset prices are unsustainable long-term---- ultimately leading to a sober correction. This is what happened in Florida as the real estate bubble burst. Many ordinary people and several investors were wiped out in this financial catastrophe.

MORAL OF THE STORY

The Florida land bubble indicates once more how strong public greed is. Everyone is seeking to gain something for nothing.

With credit access easy and the national economy progressing well, several well-intentioned and otherwise rational Americans lost their shirt yielding to irrational exuberance in the real estate market. It was nothing but a repeat of the herd mentality seen in the Dutch tulip crisis expressing itself once more in a new location in the United States. The moral of this story is that people however intelligent and rational at most times, do not change their speculative behaviors, irrespective of where they are in this world. The motivating factor of greed and instant riches is sure enough an easy reason why so many investors lose their reason and eventually take a great investment loss.

# CHAPTER 18

## THE GREAT DEPRESSION

The Great Depression was a period of severe economic contraction right through the world. Different countries were effected at different periods of each country took its own time which was from a few to several years to recover (economically). The United States took many years to get out of the negative economic effects of the Depression.

In the United States, the beginning of the Great Depression was on October 29, 1929. This date is commonly called Black Tuesday. On that one day, the stock market crashed more than 12%. The Dow Jones Industrial Average eventually bottomed out in July 1932 with a loss of approximately 89 percent value.

Most economists and historians do not agree upon the actual causes of the Great Depression and historians---- however there are a few well-known causes. Before we study these causes, it is most important to understand that the stock market crash of 1929 and the Great Depression is not one and the same thing, although the stock market crash was the first point of entry (and a preliminary cause) into this turbulent period called the Great Depression.

Other well-known causes of the Great Depression are enumerated below:

## BANK FAILURES

The Great Depression lasted for several years in the US. Great economic pain was experienced right through the 1930's until the United States was drawn into World War 2 in 1941. As general economic conditions worsened, banks could not collect on their debts in the marketplace. This resulted in the wholesale collapse of more than 9100 banks. Since there was no bank deposit insurance in those days, a bank collapsing resulted in the total loss of lifetime savings of honest customers who had trusted such banks with their hard earned money. Also, the weaker banks, which were able to weather this financial storm, started lending out less money's------ they were more concerned about their survival and started hoarding cash. Less loans to businesses resulted in less industrial and business production, leading to job retrenchments and lower consumer spending since fired workers did not have the financial wherewithal to continue purchasing numerous goods. It was a negative chain reaction and further contributed to the economic malaise.

## REDUCTION IN PURCHASES

With great financial insecurity people just started spending less since they needed to accumulate more reserves for a rainy day.

This reinforced the negative economic cycle and at its peak there were more than 25 percent of the workforce unemployed.

CHANGED NATIONAL ECONOMIC POLICY

This was a period of protectionism in the U.S. One of the protectionist tools employed by the Government was the Hawley-Smoot Tariff Act of 1930. By levying a special import tax, the Act was supposed to protect domestic American companies. But this mechanism backfired with retaliatory trade moves by the discriminated trade nations---- this all resulted in less global in less trade, creating further economic difficulties.

American exports declined from $5.2 billion in 1929 to around $1.7 billion in 1933.Hardest hit and leading in export reductions from the US were commodities like wheat, cotton, tobacco and lumber. Some historians claim that collapse of farm exports caused American farmers to default on their loans, resulting in bank instability which lead to bank runs in rural America.

DROUGHT

Several parts of the country were faced with drought and the plight of both landowners and tenant farmers were difficult as these individuals suffered tremendously since they could not plant and harvest their land in the absence of reasonable water supplies.

## REASONS ADVANCED BY FISHER

Irving Fisher in his classical presentation in October 1933 entitled "The Debt Deflation theory of Great Depressions" mentions that the predominant factor leading to the Great Depression as being over indebtedness and deflation. Fisher tied loose credit to over indebtedness, which fueled speculation and asset bubbles.

Fisher outlined nine factors interacting with one another under conditions of debt and deflation, which created the mechanics of boom to bust. This is how the chain of events expressed themselves:

1. Debt liquidation and distress selling.
2. Contraction of the money supply as bank loans are paid off.
3. A fall in the level of asset prices.
4. A still greater fall in the net worth of businesses, creating bankruptcies.
5. A fall in business profits.
6. A marked reduction in output, trade and employment.
7. Pessimism and a general lack of confidence.
8. Hoarding of money.
9. A fall in nominal interest rates and a rise in deflation adjusted interest rates.

## FDR AND THE NEW DEAL

Franklin Roosevelt became president of the United States on March 4, 1933. This was in the middle of the Depression Years. He immediately instituted what was called the New Deal. This was a group of short-term economic recovery programs, including economic aid and work assistance programs. It also involved end of the gold standard and of prohibition. This was followed by the Second New Deal programs which included more long term financial assistance involving several new government welfare and other institutions like the Social Security System, the formation of the Federal Deposit Insurance Administration, the Federal Housing administration, Fannie Mae, the Securities and Exchange Commission amongst others.

## FACTS & FIGURES ON THE GREAT DEPRESSION IN THE U.S.

Here are some facts and figures relating to the Great Depression:

1. 13 million people became unemployed.
2. Industrial production fell by nearly 45% between 1929 and 1932
3. Homebuilding dropped by 80 per cent between 1929 and 1932.
4. About 5000 banks went out of business from 1929 to 1932.

5. By 1933, 11000 out of the 25000 banks had failed in the United States.

6. In 1933, 25% of all workers and 37% of all non-farm workers were unemployed.

7. Over one million families lost their farms between 1930 and 1934.

8. Corporate profits had dropped from $10 billion dollars in 1929 to $1 billion in 1932.

9. Nine million savings accounts had been wiped out between 1930 and 1933.

10. 273,000 families had been evicted from their homes in 1932i

11. There were two million homeless people migrating around the country.

MORAL OF THE STORY

It is very important to remember and learn from the lessons of the Great Depression. Starting with a system of loose credit where money was freely available for the taking, banks encouraged a lot of loans to be taken by everyone. This period of free credit access led to massive speculation in the stock market of the day.

The run up in stock prices were not sustainable long-term leading to its collapse along with decimation of investment values.

It is critical to be aware and understand how free credit, reckless borrowing and over stimulation of the lending process by greedy bankers created a bubble of massive proportions. The bubble first burst in the stock market and then was followed by a real estate bubble resulting in great pain to all the citizens. The banking bubble burst almost at the same time as the real estate bubble. One must closely note that the stock market, the real estate market and the banking market are very closely linked. Disturbances in one market have a greater probability of crossing over and destroying another related market. This is because the source of capital for risky investments starts with the banking system. Once general credit conditions are good, banks lend capital to risk takers, who invest it in stocks or real estate for a quick profit.

Once one or the other, i.e. the stock market or real estate market goes down, banks get hurt, many failing because borrowers cannot repay their loans. Bankruptcy in  the banking sector, results in hoarding of cash by banks and less loan activity which results in a  downturn in economic activity.

It is really critical that lawmakers create both enduring legislation to put checks and controls in the lending process along with an audit of the real contents of bank balance sheets.

Also, care must be taken not only to create conditions to ensure prosperity but also to institute early warning systems to signal an oncoming tsunami. In this sense government and other banking regulators have the responsibility for controlling great excesses before it is too late by instituting and enforcing risk management systems.

# CHAPTER 19

# THE US SAVINGS AND LOANS CRISIS

Savings and loans are a form of banking organization, known as "Savings and Loans Associations". They are also commonly referred to as S&A's in the United States. These organizations have existed since the 1800's in the US. They originally served as community-based institutions for savings and mortgages. In their original intended function, their role was to attract public deposits into fixed savings products and to re-invest such proceeds into granting mortgages for real estate acquisitions.

What turned out as a very noble cause of incorporation (for S&L's) slowly disintegrated into a major financial problem in the marketplace. The savings and loans crisis of the 1980's and 1990's resulted in the failure of 747 savings and loans associations. The ultimate cost of the crisis is estimated to have totaled around $160 billion dollars of which about $125 billion dollars were paid out by the US Government. The concomitant slowdown in the finance industry and real estate market may have been an important contributor to the 1990-91 economic recession. In short, the Savings and Loans crisis created the Greatest Banking collapse and crisis since the Great Depression of 1929.

## CONTRIBUTING CAUSES OF S& L CRISIS

There were numerous causes behind the insolvency of these S&L institutions. Some notable ones are:

1) Tax Reform Act of 1986

This Act removed many tax shelters, especially for real estate investment. Very simply it restricted the amount of investment losses a real estate investor, say, could write off against his other sources of income. Many investors were attracted to real estate since it gave them an advantage tax-wise to engage in such investments. Losses incurred in real estate projects could be written off against earned income, which created a miraculous cash flow situation, since it altered the actual amount of money required to actually get involved in a real estate situation. Since the Tax Reform Act plugged this major tax advantage, investors started pulling out of new investment projects and attempted to sell current real estate holdings. This investment behavior contributed to the end of the real estate boom of the early to mid-80s and facilitated the Savings and loans crisis. 2) Deregulation

This process gave S&A's a great deal of power in choosing the kinds of investments they could engage in. In their early years, the savings and loans institutions could only take deposits from the public and that too at fixed maximum rates of interest.

Deregulation gave them inopportunity to get into businesses they were not suited to like lending money to real estate developers and direct investments in real estate in the form of land. This portfolio mix was inherently risky and with high interest rates in the environment contributed to their financial collapse.

3) Imprudent real estate lending

As mentioned above, as a result of deregulation which encouraged imprudent real estate lending, money was lent to projects whose risk was not properly measured by S&L's. William Seldmen, former chairman of the Federal Deposit Insurance Corporation and the Resolution Trust Corporation, stated," The banking problems of the '80s and'90s came primarily but not exclusively from unsound real estate lending."

4) Brokered deposits

Deposit brokers were a rare breed of agent, who charged customers commissions in exchange for finding the highest available savings rate. They also engaged in the process of actually investing this money, on the customer's behalf in CD (certificates of deposit). These CD's were usually short term in nature. Earlier banks and thrifts could only have 5 per cent of their deposit base in brokered deposits but the authorities eventually raised this limit. A small thrift could attract millions of dollars in new capital by offering ludicrously higher rates of interest.

This would mean that they would have to invest this capital in even riskier forms of investment to be able to turn out a profit. This created an opening into uncharted waters, where banks moved into an area of investment where they had no expertise and lacked adequate risk management and risk control systems to evaluate the potential loss in a new investment. This problem was exacerbated by a scam instituted by some deposit brokers into what is now known as "linked financing." In linked financing a broker would offer thrift a large sum of money as new capital deposits in exchange for such institutions provided capital to recommended borrowers. The broker made fees on attracting the capital into the thrift and again charged a hefty fee to channel new loans into recommended borrowers/clients. This process caused thrifts to be tricked into taking on bad loans. Michael Milliken of Drexel, Burnham and Lambert packaged brokered funds for several S&A's on the conditions that the institutions invest in the junk bonds of his clients.

5) End of an inflationary period.

Paul Volcker, Secretary of the Treasury in the US government made a speech of October 6,1979. His purpose for the speech was to institute a series of measures to wring inflation out of the US economy. The US then found itself subject to an orchestrated round of short-term interest rate increases with a view to controlling inflation. This led to a series of asset-liability mismatches at the thrifts.

As short-term interest rates increased, there was a mismatch in the making. Thrifts usually paid short-term market interest rates to their clients and used these funds to earn higher interest by providing loans to heir borrowers. They were therefore engaging in an interest rate risk game. As long as short-term interest rates were lower than long-term interest rates, they stood to make a profit. But with the change in the inflationary environment in the US what actually happened was that rising short-term interest rates exceeded the long-term cost of capital, a process that decimated a thrifts balance sheet. Thrifts now were running losses on their portfolios and had to engage in ever increasing risks to make some money. This steered them into the wrong direction. Zvi Bodie, professor of finance and economics at the Boston University School of Management, writing in the St. Louis Federal Reserve Review wrote, " asset liability mismatch was a principal cause of the Savings And loan crisis."

## THE ROLE OF FRAUD IN THE S & L CRISIS

As rules surrounding investment and capital-raising activities changed, the industry attracted a lot of unscrupulous entrepreneurs. Some of the better-documented investment scams were the Lincoln Savings and Loan scam and the Silverado Savings and Loan scandal. In view of the financial crisis surrounding the thrift industry, the US government started encouraging mergers and acquisitions and general restructuring of the industry.

These moves were strongly opposed by thrift owners, who resorted to political lobbying to protect their capital investments in the thrifts.

LINCOLN SAVINGS AND LOAN

Lincoln Savings and Loan was to become one of the largest thrift failures when it closed in 1989. The controller of the thrift, Charles Keating was a well-known public figure with strong political connections. In 1987, Charles Keating organized a group of US senators in senate questioning--- a process where the head of the US thrift regulatory association (FHLBB) was grilled by senators on why the regulatory body was trying to use unrequited force in the activities of Lincoln Savings and Loan. This case was muddied by the fact that Charles Keating had made a political contribution of 3,000,000 dollars to the senators and demanded (although this couldn't be proved) that the Senators support his thrift.

However, as a result of investigations into the matter, three of the senators found their political careers ended as a result and the other two were rebuked by the Senate Ethics committee for exercising" poor judgment" for intervening with the federal regulators on behalf of Keating.

## SILVERADO SAVINGS AND LOAN

Silverado Savings and Loan collapsed in 1988. Cost to the taxpayers for their bailout amounted to around 1.3 billion dollars. Neil Bush was Director of Silverado at the time. Neil was accused of giving himself a loan from Silverado, but he denied all wrongdoing.

The US office of thrift supervision investigated Silverado's failure and determined that Neil Bush had engaged in numerous "breaches of his fiduciary duties involving multiple conflicts of interest." Although Bush was not indicted on criminal charges, the Federal Deposit insurance corporation brought a civil action against him and the other Silverado directors this was eventually settled out of court, with Bush paying 50,000dollars as part of the settlement, the Washington Post reported. As the director of the failed thrift, Bush voted to approve 100 million dollars in what was to become a bad loan to his two business partners. And in voting for the loans, he failed to inform these fellow board members at Silverado that the loan applicants were his business partners. A Resolution Trust Corporation lawsuit suit against Bush and other offices of Silverado was settled in 1991 for 26.5 million dollars.

## FAILURE OF REGULATORY AUTHORITIES IN S & L CRISIS

As investment rules changed, the authorities simply failed to monitor the balance sheets of thrifts. By giving them a mandate to invest on par with the banks, the authorities did not understand that they were exposing these financial institutions to great risks. As the crisis developed, instead of quickly solving the problems and closing down institutions quickly, several amendments and policy changes were made, hoping that the problem would go away. With poor regulatory oversight and lax risk management controls, this called for a recipe for disaster. Between 1986-1995 over 1000 banks with total assets over 500 billion dollars failed. By 1999, the total cost of the S & L crisis was over 150 billion dollars.

## MORAL OF THE STORY

The S & L Crisis again demonstrates how greed caused great problems and a total failure in protecting the savings of the common man. As greedy businesspeople got into opening a new S & A or purchasing an existing thrift they became beneficiaries of millions of dollars of public money, which instead of being invested responsibly went into questionable investments in real estate and land purchase and financing of developers. With no proper risk control models nor any concern for the future of these investments except to line their pockets, here was a financial system which had gone totally crazy and out of logical control.

Owners of thrifts milked the business system—they saw an unprecedented opportunity to attract funds for their own businesses. In some cases, like the Bush fiasco, directors siphoned public money in a thrift into their own pocket indirectly like directing 100 million dollars into a business loan taken out surreptitiously by two of his business partners.

Was this not an easy way of attracting 100 million dollars into a public venture? And what was the loss if the company who took this 100 million dollar loan went belly up? Not much really--- the company would declare bankruptcy and then the legal process would have to sort out the various villains- in the meantime these business villains due to their political and corporate position got to fraudulently use public money to fuel private greed.

The Savings and Loan Crisis also saw the total abandonment of government responsibility to monitor the financial institutions themselves. With budget cuts and fewer regulatory personnel, there was no national, business or political will to control the problem quickly. This crisis indicated the need for more closer government regulation and government sponsored risk-monitoring systems. Unfortunately we still have not learned the value of more government regulation and enforcements as these greedy business lords continue to plunder the financial system--- a fact well noted in the great financial and credit crisis of 2007.

# CHAPTER 20

# THE REAL ESTATE & STOCK MARKET BUBBLE
# IN JAPAN
# (1985-1989)

The Japanese asset price bubble was an economic bubble, which lasted from 1985 to 1989. There was a run-up of real estate and stock market prices during this period, finally leading up to the stock market crash after the end of 1989. Before this stock market crash, the Nikkei stock index, a barometer of frequently traded Japanese stocks, hits its all time high on December 29,1989 when it reached an intra-day high of 38957.44 before closing at 38,915.87.

## HISTORY OF STOCK MARKET AND REAL ESTATE BUBBLE

In the decades following their defeat in World War 2, the Japanese Government had an ambitious plan of rebuilding their war-torn economy. With Hiroshima and Nagasaki blown into smithereens by nuclear attacks from the US, Japan implemented stringent tariffs and policies to encourage their citizens to save their income. As citizens started pouring their hard-earned savings in banks and other local financial institutions, the bloated capital base of banks allowed them to  loan out even more money to small and medium sized businesses. Credit to the average Japanese Joe Bloe also became easier to obtain.

Japan started developing huge trade surpluses with their trading partners and the yen continued to appreciate against other currencies. With cheaper and more ready access to credit, Japanese companies were able to reduce their unit prices of production (as their cost of capital was reduced) and this widened the trade surplus further as these companies were able to capture more of the world's export market. And with the yen continuing its upward appreciation, financial assets in Japan became very attractive. With so much surplus cash and potential profit, the financial environment was ripe for speculation.

As the stock market values kept rising, banks to exacerbate the problem started lending out more money in the form of risky loans; some of these loans were to finance the purchase of more stocks and some of the money found itself lent for the purpose of speculative real estate investments. So speculative was the market in 1989, that choice properties in the upscale Ginza district of Tokyo were commanding a premium of over 100 million yen (around 1 million dollars) per square meter. This translated to a value of around $93000 per square feet, in American terms.

But this speculative fever and run up in stock and real estate prices could not lost forever. When the market crashed, it real came down with a big bang. At its worst, residential homes in Tokyo dropped by around 90 per cent and prime "A" (the choicest and most expensive) property in Tokyo's financial districts had slumped to less than one percent of its peak. The stock market also went through a major downward correction.

However, this problem did not go away fast. The easily obtainable credit that helped create the real estate bubble continued to be major problem for many years to come.

After the bubble burst, many events occurred gradually rather than catastrophically, and the decade following the bubble is commonly referred to as Japan's lost decade or end of the century in Japan.

MORAL OF THE STORY

As in past financial catastrophes noted in this book, the combination of risky lending, numerous speculators and their targeted stock and real estate market bore the seeds of a great financial disaster waiting to happen. History has a way of repeating itself even at different periods in different parts of the world. The sequences of events were as follows:

1. **Run up in real estate and stock market prices** followed by introduction of
2. **Speculators** whose greed fueled the relentless purchase of numerous real estate properties and stocks, with the sole intention of making a fast buck and flipping the asset for a magnificent profit, which process was aided by
3. **Banks**, who in their turn were greedy to increase profits by granting reckless and high risk loans.

This bubble of higher and higher real estate and stock market prices went up so high that it had to burst and when it burst it dragged not only the real estate and stock market values but also the rest of the economy. Personal greed financed by public money financed by unconscionable banks, created massive wealth destruction and crossed from the decimation of financial assets to the rest of the real economy.

# CHAPTER 21

## THE REAL ESTATE & STOCK MARKET BUBBLE IN SCANDINAVIA (1985-1989)

Around the time Japan was going through a crisis, Sweden, a big Scandinavian country situated thousands of miles away, was going through a financial crisis of its own.

For those of you who are not familiar with Sweden, this is a Nordic country on the Scandinavian Peninsula in Northern Europe. Sweden has land borders with Norway to the west and Finland to the northeast and the Oresund Bridge in the South connect it to Denmark. At 450,000 sq. kilometers, Sweden is the third largest country in the European Union with a total population of over 9 million people.

Sweden experienced a bursting real estate bubble. This bubble was caused by inadequate controls on lending combined with an international recession and a policy switch from anti-unemployment policies to anti-inflationary policies, which resulted in a major financial crisis in the early 1990s.

The problem first started with deregulation of the country's credit market in 1985. With a lot of money floating around accompanied with reckless and low quality loans provided by banks to speculators---the situation became ripe for years of unbridled and crazy property speculation. The speculation was predominantly focused on commercial real estate investments. When the bubble burst, everything was affected.

Property prices came down dramatically and a lot of banks were left holding mortgage security for their loans, which was now worth way less than the original loan provided. The banks experienced great depletion of capital in their balance sheet as a result. This sparked the banking crisis in Sweden. According to the Swedish central bank, " a wave of bankruptcies" between 1990 and 1994 left Sweden's seven largest banks, which accounted for 90% of the market, with loan losses totaling the equivalent of 12 percent of Sweden's annual gross domestic product. As further reported by the Local newspaper, Sweden's news in English, the center right government in Sweden took a hands-on approach, pumping cash into the banks deemed to only have temporary problems and letting the ones believed to have no prospect of viability to go under. Two banks were taken over completely by the state, which in turn offered a blanket guarantee to all creditors, but not for the shareholders. This credit guarantee made it possible for everyone to do business with the banks without any kind of risk.

The Swedish state took over insecure loans during the crisis worth around 10 billion dollars of taxpayer money, but eventually got most of it back through dividends and later reselling the nationalized banks assets.

MORAL OF THE STORY

Once again loose, high-risk, unconscionable lending by banks with commercial real estate acquisitions as the target resulted in a run up of prices.

The real estate bubble resulted in a massive loss to Swedish banks when it burst thereby creating a banking crisis. In this case, the culprit was speculative fever in real estate aided by greedy bankers and overzealous money-hungry investors.

However, where this story ends differently is that the steps taken by the Swedish Government helped stabilize this crisis with relatively little cost to the exchequer and taxpayer. The Government in Sweden had the audacity to let very weak banks go under immediately and instituted strict terms for release of capital into the insolvent banking system. They did this by acquiring ownership interest in the banks themselves(by becoming common shareholders) with a view to recovering their investment when the investment scenario improved. By extracting strong commitments from existing bank shareholders and carefully monitoring lending and other speculative activities, the government was able to create a sense of confidence in the mind of the investment public. Also by immediately guaranteeing capital to all creditors of the banks , the government created a no-risk environment for all creditors of the various insolvent banks. When conditions improved they sold assets and recovered their investments.

The United States has a lot to learn from the Swedish model of government action, which swiftly and courageously stabilized the banking crisis and restored immense confidence in the minds of everyone.

# CHAPTER 22

# THE ASIAN FINANCIAL CRISIS OF 1997

In an article by Kim, Suk H. and Haque, Mahfuzul entitled, " Asian financial crisis of 1997: Causes and policy responses", published by the Multinational Business Review, Spring 2002 Issue----- a brilliant analysis is made of the causes, effects and consequences of the Asian financial crisis. This article is being used as a major reference source for this chapter, along with a list of references at the end of this chapter.

For years, East-Asian countries were held up as economic Icons. Their typical blend of high savings and Investment rates, autocratic political systems, export-oriented businesses, restricted domestic markets, government capital allocation, and controlled financial systems were hailed as the Ideal recipe for strong economic growth of developing counties (Shapiro, 1999). However, in July 1997, currency turmoil erupted In Thailand. This currency crisis spread from there to Indonesia and Korea, then to Russia, then to Latin America. Few countries have not been touched by the global forces that this crisis--some accounts the worst since the 1980s debt crisis--has unleashed.

Professor Paul Krugman who threw cold water on the popular enthusiasm on the Asian success story even before the crisis said, "I was 90 percent wrong about what was going to happen, but everyone else was 150 percent wrong. They only saw the miracle and one of the risk."

RECENT INTERNATIONAL FINANCIAL CRISES

The 1997 Asian crisis is the 4th international financial crisis. The first major blow to the international financial system took place in August 1982, when Mexico announced that it could not meet its regularly scheduled payments to international creditors. Shortly thereafter, Brazil and Argentina were in the same situation. By Spring 1983, about 25 developing countries could not make regularly scheduled payments and negotiated rescheduling with creditor banks. These countries accounted for two-thirds of the total debt owed by non-oil developing countries to private banks at the time.

The second crisis occurred in the fall of 1992, when a wave of speculative attacks hit the European Monetary System (EMS). Before the end of the year, five countries-- Finland, the United Kingdom, Italy, Sweden, and Norway had floated their currencies. Despite attempts by a number of other countries to remain in the EMS by devaluing their currencies (Spain, Portugal, and Ireland), the old system was ultimately unsalvageable. The bands of the EMS were widened from +/- 2.25 percent to +/- 115 percent in August 1993.

The third crisis came on December 20, 1994 when the Mexican government announced its decision to devalue the peso against the dollar by 14 percent. This decision, however, touched off a panic situation to sell pesos, thereby compelling the Mexican government to float the peso. A rash of speculative attacks against other Latin American currencies--Argentina (peso), Brazil (real), Peru (new sol), and Venezuela (Bolivar)--broke out immediately through what became known as the tequila effect. Several non-Latin American countries, Thailand, Hong Kong, the Philippines, and Hungary suffered brief speculative attacks. However, only few countries actually devalued their currencies. Argentina was the only other country that suffered a sharp recession as a result of the Mexican peso crisis.

The Asian crisis of 1997, despite prompt and concerted action by developing countries, industrialized countries, and international organizations to contain it, quickly and ferociously spread to north Asian, latin, and eastern European economies to varying degrees. In fact, this Asian crisis had pushed one-third of the globe into recession during 1998. The crisis has raised a variety of questions not only about the future of the region's economy, but also about the impact of the crisis on multinational companies and the world economy.

All four crisis episodes occurred under fixed exchange rate regimes. Economic theory suggests that a pegged exchange rate regime can become vulnerable when cross-border capital flows are highly mobile. A central bank that pegs its exchange rate to a hard currency implicitly guarantees that any investors can exchange their local currency assets for that hard currency at the prevailing exchange rate. If investors suspect that the government will not or cannot maintain the peg, they may flee the currency; this capital flight, in turn, deletes hard currency reserves and force the devaluation they fear.

Financial crises have taken three main forms: currency crises and banking crises, or both (Kaminsky and Reinhard 1997) Currency crises are usually attacks on the domestic currency that end with a large fall in its value. Banking crises refer to bank runs or other events that lead to closure, merger, takeover, or large-scale assistance by the government to financial institutions. Sometimes, both banking and currency crises occur around the same time--the so-called twin crises. The 1997 Asian crisis is the most recent example of twin crises. Five East-Asian countries--Indonesia, Korea, Malaysia, Philippines, and Thailand experienced currency turbulence along with serious banking sector problems. Earlier examples of twin crises include Argentina (1981), Uruguay (1982), and Chile (1982). More recently, Mexico (1994), Argentina (1995), Brazil (1998), and Russia (1998) experienced similar problems.

The rest of paper is organized as follows. The first section discusses how an economic crisis in an emerging economy such as Thailand could spread throughout the world. The second section describes how and how much capital flows went in and out of East Asia. The third section analyzes the causes of the Asian crisis. The last section lists policy responses to this crisis.

## AN ECONOMIC CRISIS IN THAILAND SPREAD THROUGHOUT THE WORLD

International capital flows caused "booms and busts" for Thailand's economy. How could an economic crisis in an emerging economy such as Thailand could spread throughout the world. Thailand's economy surged until early 1997 partly because the Thais found they could borrow money at low interest rates overseas, in dollars, more cheaply than they could at home, in baht. By late 1996, foreign investors began to move their money out of Thailand because they worried about Thais' ability to repay. In February 1997, foreign investors and Thai companies rushed to convert their baht to dollars. The Thai central bank responded by buying baht with its dollar reserves and raising interest rates.

The rise in interest rates drove down prices for stocks and land. This dynamic situation drew attention to serious problems in the Thai economy: the huge foreign debt, trade deficits, and a banking system weakened by a heavy burden of unpaid loans.

The Thai central bank ran out of dollars to support the baht. On July 2, the central bank stopped to defend the baht's fixed value against the dollar. And then the currency lost 16 percent of its value in one day.

Investors and companies in the Philippine, Malaysia, Indonesia, and Korea realized that these economies shared all of Thailand's problems. So, investors and companies rushed to convert local currencies into dollars. And then, the peso, ringgit, Rupiah, and won toppled in value like dominos in a row. In the fourth quarter of 1997, the International Monetary Fund (IMF) arranged emergency rescue packages of $18 billion for Thailand, $43 billion for Indonesia, and $58 billion for Korea.

By the end of 1998, the Asian crisis of 1997 spread to Russia, Brazil, and many other countries. Again, the IMF arranged bailout packages of $23 billion for Russia in July 1998 and $42 for Brazil in November 1998. This means that since mid-summer 1997, IMF-led rescue packages for Asia, Russia, and Brazil racked up a total of some $184 billion to keep world markets safe.

In theory, capital is a boom, enabling developing countries to reduce poverty and raise living standards. But the theory does not always work smoothly. Countries mismanage the inflows. Banks can be ripe with favoritism or incompetence; bad loans are made. Moreover, multinational companies may build too many factories.

Speculation may also propel stock prices to unrealistic heights. Last, ample foreign exchange provided by overseas investors may support a spending spree on imports.

If capital inflows slow or reverse, the boom can collapse. This is precisely what happened in Thailand, where the Asian crisis started. The construction of unneeded office buildings was halted; bad loans mushroomed at finance companies and banks; and the stock market dived. Similar problems afflicted other Asian economies, and losses extended to their foreign trading partners and investors beyond Asia.

There are a number of plausible answers to the question of why the dominos toppled in rapid succession, even though in some cases, they were nowhere near each other (Phillips, 1999). Countries are increasingly connected by trade and investment, so a downturn in one hurts exports and investment of another. Countries also compete against one another. When one country devalues its currency, others can feel pressured to do the same in order to keep their exports and inward investment competitive. Commodity prices provide another link among troubled economies. For example, as Asia sank into recession, its businesses and consumers cut their purchases of oil. That, in turn, accelerated the collapse in the price of crude oil and slashed the revenue for oil exporting countries such as Russia. Russia being a minor player in the league of oil exporting countries is a price taker and not a price setter.

# Asian financial crisis of 1997: Causes and policy responses

## INTERNATIONAL CAPITAL FLOWS IN AND OUT OF THE ASIA

The greater integration of emerging market countries with international capital markets has brought problems as well as benefits for recipients. On the one hand, access to foreign funds has helped finance economic development. On the other hand, greater integration has rendered developing countries more vulnerable to the effects of capital flow reversals, whether due to bad policies or speculation. This vulnerability is highlighted by the Asian crisis of 1997 (Aybar and Milman, 1999). As one observer puts it, "Capital flows around the world are like oceanic tides: in deep bays, tidal movements are little noticed, but in shallow bays, the ebb and flows of the global ocean create huge effect." Paul Volcker, former chairman of the U..S. Federal Reserve System, puts it in a different way, "Small and open economies are inherently vulnerable to the volatility of global capital markets."

As shown in Table 1, for several years before the outbreak of the crisis, the five Asian countries hit hardest by the crisis--Indonesia, Korea, Malaysia, the Philippines, and Thailand--enjoyed an enormous inflow of foreign capital Line 2 of Table 1), mostly from private sources (Line 3). Most of these private flows came as loans from private creditors (Line 7), such as commercial banks and non-bank creditors. In fact, these inflows tripled in just two years from $25.8 billion in 1994 to $83.5 billion.

This foreign capital inflow enabled these countries to finance their current account deficits (Line 1), invest overseas (Line 13), and add to their reserves (Line 14). In 1995, for example, $81.5 billion flowed into these five countries from international source; $41 billion financed the current account deficit and $26.5 billion was reinvested in non-equity assets overseas. The remaining $14 billion went into the countries' international reserves.

In 1995 and 1996, the bulk of these inflows were from private sources. Official inflows (Line 10)-- loans and other financing from international organizations such as the World Bank and the IF (Line 11), as well as assistance from other nations ( Line 12) were either negligible and even negative. That is, the countries were paying back international official creditors.

However, the sharp reversal of capital flows to East Asia in the second half of 1997 is clearly evident in the data. External financing to the five countries dropped from $106.6 billion in 1996 to $28.8 billion in 1997--an amount insufficient to cover the countries' collective current account deficits at the time. Private flows (Line 3) turned from an inflow of $103.2 billion in 1996 to an outflow of $1.1 billion in 1997. This turnaround of $101.7 billion in one year (actually just six months) was equivalent to about 10 percent of the combined GDP of these five countries. Reserves fell by almost $35.2 billion as the countries attempted to defend their currencies and bolster their economies.

Official capital flows, meanwhile, jumped significantly to help cover the short-fall and moderate the crisis.

CAUSES OF THE CRISIS: TWO THEORIES

During the second half of 1997, currencies and stock markets plunged across East Asia, while hundreds of banks, builders, and manufacturers went bankrupt. More specifically, currency values and stock prices of these five Asian countries fell from 40 percent to 80 percent a piece from July 1997 to early 1998 (Pettway, 1999). This crisis in Asia caught nearly everyone by surprise because Asia's fundamentals looked very good. However, investors and policy makers failed to recognize a number of similarities between the period preceding the Asian crisis and the period leading up to the two previous developing country crises: the 1980s Latin American debt crisis and the1994-95 Mexican financial crisis. First, capital inflows to five East-Asian countries were extremely heavy prior to the downturns as international investors enjoyed easier access to domestic financial markets. As in the prior two crises, spreads on Asian emerging market debt declined substantially as investors downgraded the risk difference between developed countries' and Asian emerging market countries' debt. Second, these countries enjoyed strong ratings from international creditor agencies and widespread investor participation in their markets. In Asia, as in the previous two crises, both of these two factors could be viewed as very positive developments.

However, as in the prior two crises, there were warning signs that all of the confidence in Asia may have been misplaced. Most domestic borrowers, for example, were unhedged against exchange rate risk, making them to increase their foreign debt load significantly when a borrowing country's exchange rate changes dramatically. Furthermore, Asian financial institutions had borrowed a significant amount of external liquid liabilities that were not backed by liquid assets, making them vulnerable to panics (Moreno, 1998).

The causes of the Asian crisis include governments' futile attempts to keep their currencies at artificially high levels; government-directed banking systems and lending decisions; crony capitalism; massive overinvestment by corporations funded by excessive borrowing; the lack of transparency that masked the extent of problems they developed; inadequate financial regulation and supervision; labor market "rigidities", and a pronounced mismatch in the duration of assets and liabilities in both the corporate and banking sectors (E. Han Kim, 1998).

Perhaps the biggest contributor to the Asian financial crisis of 1997 is its gross misallocation of capital and human resources, combined with a flagrant disregard for the bottom line. This misallocation of capital and human resources caused by the lack of corporate governance had resulted in the widespread value destruction by Asian companies, which in turn had led to a lower value for the overall economy and weakened the banking sector.

Underlying all of these weaknesses were pervasive moral hazard-- "heads I win, tails someone else loses" philosophy. Banks, investors, and business firms assumed that governments and international organizations would bail them out in the event of financial catastrophe. Such a moral hazard had created incentives for risky behavior on the part of developing countries and international investors.

Neely (1999) argues that "although many explanations have been offered as the causes of the Asian crisis, the vast majority of views fall into one of two theories: the fundamentalist view and the panic view." The fundamentalist view focuses on how borrowing countries' policies and practices fed the crisis, whereas the panic view focuses on the role lenders played. The following two sections depends heavily upon Neely's article.

The Fundamentalist View: The fundamentalist view holds that flawed financial systems were at the root of the crisis and its spread. The seeds for the financial crisis were actually shown several years before currency pressures began. Most East-Asian countries had tied their currencies to the dollar. This tie served them well until 1995 because it promoted low inflation, supported currency stability, and boosted exports. However, the appreciation of the dollar against the yen and other major currencies since 1995 caused East Asian countries to lose their competitiveness in export markets.

The crash of world trade in 1996 after two years of rapid growth also affected the Asian markets. From April 1995, the US dollar appreciated continuously and significantly. The dollar linked Asian currencies appreciated accordingly and this made their exports uncompetitive leading to large currency account deficits (see Table 1). Thus, the US dollar appreciation in 1995-97 contributed to 1997 financial crisis. This is similar to the situation in the late 1970s and 1980s when increased interest rates contributed significantly to the Latin American debt crisis.

Meanwhile, the maturity mismatch and the currency mismatch --the use of short-term debt for fixed assets and unhedged external debt--made banks and firms vulnerable to sudden swings in international investors' confidence. Many economists believe that these two types of mismatch were caused by moral hazard because most East-Asian companies and financial institutions operated with implicit or explicit government guarantees.

An increasing portion of foreign capital inflows to the region consisted of liquid portfolio investment (short-term bank loans and security investment) rather than long-term direct investment. Most of these liquid capital flows were directed into long-term, risky investments, such as real estate. Frequently, these same assets were used for collateral and investment, driving the value of existing collateral up, which in turn spurred more lending and increased asset prices.

Risk was further heightened by when local banks--in response to low interest rates abroad and fixed exchange rates at home--began to borrow foreign exchange abroad. These local banks converted the foreign exchange to domestic currency and lent the proceeds to their domestic customers in domestic currency, thereby assuming all the exchange rate risk. Dumside, Eichenbaum, and Robelo (1998) provide evidences that the poor quality of bank assets was well known months or even before the devaluation that marked the beginning of the crisis. Their model implies that the Thai devaluation could have been foreseen over two years before the devaluation occurred.

The absence of the macroeconomic imbalances typical of past crises led some to argue that the Asian crisis was not caused by problems with the economic fundamentals. Rather, a swift change in expectations was the catalyst for the massive capital outflows that triggered the crisis. The panic view holds that problems in Thailand were turned into the Asian crisis because of international investors' irrational behavior and the overly harsh fiscal and momentary policies prescribed by the International Monetary Fund ()Mil) as the crisis broke.

Several factors support the premise that the crisis was panic-induced. First, there were no warning signs, such as an increase in interest rates on the region's debt or downgrading on the region's debt by debt rating agencies.

Second, prior to the crisis, international banks made substantial loans to private firms and banks that did not have any sort of government guarantees or insurance. This fact contradicts the idea that moral hazard was so pervasive so that investors knowingly made bad deals, assuming that they would be bailed out. It is consistent, however, with the notion that international investors panicked in unison and withdrew money from all investments--good or bad.

Third, once the crisis was under way, the affected countries experienced widespread credit crunches. For example, even viable domestic exporters with confirmed sales could not get credit, again suggesting irrationality on the part of lenders. Finally, the trigger for the crisis was not the deflation of asset values, as the fundamentalists argue, but the sudden withdrawal of funds from the region triggered the crisis. Radelet and Sachs (1998) argue that some of the conditions the IMF imposed on these crisis countries for financial assistance added to, rather than alleviated, the panic.

A key feature of the crises since the 1980s has been the existence of contagion or spillover effect. The panic view is consistent with the concept of "contagion", which defined as "co-movements of markets not traceable to common co-movements of fundamentals (Wolf, 1997)." In all three crisis episodes of the 1990s, a crisis that began in one country quickly spread beyond its borders.

In some cases the next victims were neighbors and trade partners; in others they were countries that shared similar policies or suffered common economic shocks. At times, as in the summer of 1998, changes in investor sentiment and increased aversion to risk contributed to contagion within and across regions.

Three channels may help to explain such contagion effects. A first channel is heard behavior, attributed to imperfect information problems. Institutional fund managers often follow investment trends of other investors to protect themselves from being blamed in the event of losses for not following trends. Another interpretation is that investors may not discriminate among different fundamentals across markets and regard emerging-market investments as an asset class. A second channel is portfolio allocation: any shock that leads to changes in asset returns in one emerging market will contribute to changes in portfolio allocation to all other emerging markets. A third channel is portfolio interdependence. In response to large capital losses in one country, a sell-off of holdings in other markets occurs in an effort to raise cash to meet investor redemptions. These channels suggest why financial markets have recently become more closely integrated and why shocks have been rapidly transmitted in global financial markets.

## POLICY RESPONSES

Regardless of the cause of the crisis and its consequent spillover to other countries, all analysts agree that the fallout in Asia and other emerging markets have been severe. Although initially only financial in nature, the crisis has led to significant real economic losses in these formerly fast-growing economies. Just like the previous developing-country crises, lenders, borrowers, and international financial institutions worked together to overcome the crisis. The external payments situation were stabilized through IMF-led aid programs, the rescheduling of short-term foreign debts, and reductions in foreign borrowing through painful reversals of current account deficits. Financial packages are now being geared to encourage the adoption of policies that could prevent crises in selected developing countries. Backed by a recent IMF quota increase of $90 billion, the IMF would make a continent short-term line of credit available before a crisis breaks out, but only if a country adopts certain policies that would limits its vulnerability. This line of credit is expected to be of short-term and charge interest rates above market rates to discourage misuse (Moreno, 1999).

East-Asian countries closed many ailing banks, cleaned up non-performing loans, encouraged surviving banks to merge with other banks, and compelled these banks to meet the capital adequacy ratio set by the Bank for International Settlements.

Corporate sector reforms included capital structure improvement through debt reduction, business restructuring to remove excess capacity, the reorientation of conglomerates on core specialists, and the upgrading of corporate governance standards. These countries also implemented market-opening measures to facilitate foreign investment.

These and other policy responses strengthened financial systems, enhanced transparency of policies and economic data, restored economic competitiveness, and modernized legal and regulatory environment for more stringent regulatory oversight and consistent application of accounting standards. The Asian crisis, like the Latin American debt crisis and the Mexican crisis, have had a profound impact not only on the economies of the affected countries, but also on the developing countries. Our analysis in this paper sheds light on the Asian countries' reversal of economic fortune and suggests action that may help countries to face and weather out the financial storms in the future."

REFERENCES

C. Bulent Aybar and Claudio D. Milman, "Globalization, Emerging Market Conditions and Currency Crisis in Asia: Implications of economic Reform and Development," Multinational Business Review, Fall 1999, pp. 37-44.

Raig Burnside, Martin Eichenbaum, and Sergio Rebelo, "Prospective Deficits and the Asian Currency Crisis," Federal Reserve Bank of

Chicago Working Paper Number WP 98-5, 1998.

Thomas J. Connelly, "The Great Asian Fire Drill," Journal of Financial Planning, April 1998, pp. 32-37. The International Monetary Fund, International Financial Statistics, various issues.

SaKong Il, "Asian Crisis Touches All in a Global Village," Business Korea, December 1998. "The IMF's Role in the International Monetary System and Financial Crisis," 15 pages from the Internet.

G. Ip, "SEC Clears Plan Tying Trade Halts to Percentage Falls, The Wall Street Journal, April 13, 1998, p. C6.

D. Catlike, "Wall Street's wobble Was at odds with what seems to be a strong economy," Time, November 10, 1997, pp. 37-39.

Gopal Garuda, "Lender of Last Resort," Harvard International Review, Summer 1998, pp. 3639.

Graciela L. Kaminsky and Carmen Reinhard, "The Twin Crises: The Causes of Banking and Balance-of-Payments Problems," Working Papers in International Economics 37, University of Maryland, Department of Economics, December, 1997.

E. Han Kim, "Globalization of Capital Markets and the Asian Financial crisis," Journal of Applied Corporate Finance, Fall 1998, pp. 30–39.

Paul Krugman, "Asia: What Went Wrong," Fortune, March 2, 1998, p. 32.

Eddy Lee, "The Asian Financial Crisis: Origins and Social Outlook," International Labor Review, March 1998, pp. 81–93.

Linda Lim, "The Southeast Asian Currency Crisis and its Aftermath," Journal of Asian Business, November 4, 1997, pp. 65 83.

Ramon Moreno, "Dealing with Currency Crises," FRBSF Economic Letter, Number 99–11, April 2, 1999.

Ramon Moreno, "What Caused East Asia's Financial Crisis," FRBSF Economic Newsletter, Federal Reserve Bank of San Francisco, Number 98–24, August 7, 1998.

Rakesh Mohan, "Striking at the Roots," Far Eastern Economic Review December 1998.

Michelle C. Neely, "Paper Tigers? How the Asian

Economies Lost Their Bite," The Regional Economist, The Federal Reserve Bank of St. Louis, January 1999, pp. 5–9.

Richard H. Pettway, "Asian Financial Crisis: The Role of China and Japan in the Post Asian Crisis Ear," Multinational Business Review, Fall 1999, pp. 13–21.

Michael M. Phillips, "Global Investing," The Wall Street Journal, April 26, 1999, Section R. R.R. Samuelson, "Global Boom and Bust,"

Newsweek November 10, 1997, p. 35. Alan C. Shapiro, Multinational Financial Management, Upper Saddle River, NJ: Prentice Hall, 1999, Chapter 1.

R. Frederick and J. Thompson, Draft OECD Principles of Corporate Governance, April 1994, 24 pages from the OECD Web Site.

Steven Radelet and Jeffrey Sachs, "The Onset of the East Asian Currency Crisis," NBER Working Paper No. 6680, April 1998.

Steven Radelet and Jeffrey Sachs, "The East Asian Financial Crisis: Diagnosis, Remedies, and Prospects," Bookings Papers on Economic Activity, 1998, Volume 1, pp. 1–74.

M. Schuman, "South Korean Banks Post $12.32 Billion Loss," The Wall Street Journal, January 20, 1999, p. A13.

Holger F. Wolf, "Regional Contagion Effects in Emerging Stock Markets," Working Papers in International Economics, G-97-03-18, Department of Economics, Princeton University, October 1997.

The World Bank, Global Economic Prospects. various issues. The World Bank, Global Development Finance, various issues.

Suk H. Kim and Mahfuzul Haque, University of Detroit, Mercy.

## MORAL OF THE STORY

The Asian crisis was a combination of a currency and financial crisis. Lessons learnt here are the disadvantages of pegging a country's currency to the US dollar, particularly when the dollar becomes stronger. This invariably leads to a non-competitiveness export wise for developing countries. Secondly, the lack of appropriate risk management with respect to currencies borrowed in US dollars and Euros could bode bad news for developing countries. With this comes the responsibility to hedge currency(borrowed) risks and set appropriate structures for bank regulation. In the future, developing countries would do better by developing better risk practice and governments should exert strong audit control of the balance sheets of banks, particularly bank's behavior is terms of lending money to the public. This is happening in Japan as late as March 2009, where the Government has sent auditors to analyze bank balance sheets to see if they are fulfilling their social responsibilities by lending to a cross section of individuals, small and medium sized businesses or whether they are merely hoarding and speculating on capital.

# CHAPTER 23

# THE NASDAQ BUBBLE IN THE UNITED STATES 1995-2000

The NASDAQ bubble is also referred to as the dot-com bubble. This bubble covered the period starting in 1995 and ending around 2000. The dot-com bubble had all to do with the new internet age. The Internet had revolutionized ways of communicating and doing business and several companies, both hardware and software-oriented started developing businesses to better capitalize on this new Internet technology.

During this momentous period, several companies became prominent. One such company was Google, which launched a search engine process, and Amazon.com, which wanted to be the world largest, and biggest online book retailer. There were a myriad of other companies who sought to capitalize on the Internet as a way of boosting corporate revenue and profits.

The public initially were skeptical but with time started embracing these companies. As a result, stock prices increased. As it happens every time, increase in stock prices at an exponential rate attracted speculators, who regular started bidding up the prices of these dot-com shares, with a view to maximize their short-term profit.

## GROWTH OF THE INTERNET BUBBLE

Venture capitalists (VC's), a special breed of financiers, who "seed" capital for new business projects, saw the opportunity to support such new Internet start-ups. They would normally fund upfront a certain amount of the start-up and development costs of the company in exchange for a percentage of profits or company shares. These venture capitalists were gambling on the success of these companies. If such companies could even start getting on their feet, the venture capitalists would create an initial public offering (IPO) of shares of such new companies. If they were able to successfully execute an IPO they would sell out their ownership position in such company--- thereby effectively cashing out on the new companies success in raising money from the public. Since the environment saw a public acceptance of these new start-ups, the venture capitalists saw it economically profitable to support many such new start-ups with the hope that they would make money through some of these ventures. Therefore the VCs had a lot to do with providing the financing, which in many cases turned out to be highly dubious and speculative---- and such investments fueled this crisis going forward.

## ADVERTISING AND MARKETING POWER

In an effort to increase their brand awareness, numerous start-ups spent several million dollars in sponsoring sporting events over television among other things. In January 2000, seventeen dot com companies each paid two million dollars for a thirty second spot on super bowl XXXIV.

What spurred this upward growth in dot com company's success was a new public awareness and acceptance of the "growth over profits" mentality. Traditionally stocks were being evaluated on a price to earnings ratio. That is, the stock price assigned by the market to a specific company stock was a function of the stock price multiplied by the multiplier of the earning on it. For example, a stock with a price-earnings ratio of 11 meant that the market was willing to value (and pay for) the stock at 11 times its current earnings per share. However, with the new dot coms there were no immediate earnings and therefore there was no way to scientifically and appropriately value them. This is where the "growth over earnings" story came in. The future growth anticipated would more than compensate for lack of earnings today and also any current annual losses. Therefore, there was no proper evaluation system in place for these stocks. This was a perfect and ripe market for speculators to step in. They sold the "growth over earnings" story well and increased their positions by huge purchases of stock---- this demand greatly increased the share prices of these stocks and contributed to the bubble.

Cities all across the United States tried to become the next Silicon Valley by building network enabled office space. Communication providers went into a lot of debt by investing in networks with high-speed equipment and fiber optic cables.

Similarly in Europe, many mobile operators spent a ton of money on 3G licenses in Germany, Italy and the United Kingdom and these investments put them into massive debt.

THE BUBBLE BURST

As with all bubbles, this high tech bubble had to burst, sooner or later. The Federal Reserve in the United States increased interest rates six times between 1999 and early 2000 and the ever expanding US economy was beginning to lose steam. The dot come bubble burst, numerically, on March 10,2000 when the technology heavy NASDAQ Composite index peaked at 5048.62 more than double its value a year ago. At its worst position the dot.com bubble caused more than a 80% depreciation in stocks of such internet companies. Even as of today, some nine years after the bubble burst, the NASDAQ QQQ stock which represents the entire internet market is at least fifty percent less than its peak achieved in March 2000.

## MORAL OF THE STORY

Here is another story where massive speculation in a new industry caused great damage to both large financial institutions and small investors alike. With a view to avoiding such costly investment mistakes in the future, investors should in the future exercise great caution and discretion in their investment review of any new promising industry like the dot.com business and be wary of corporations who are market priced on future growth as compared to hard tangible revenue results today. Also investors should be suspect of any m massive run-ups in any asset class in the investment universe. This happened clearly in the dot-cum bubble where asset value doubled in just one year. It is always better to stay with well-known brand names with a predictable cash flow stream then new arrivals with no real income story.

The moral of the dot-com bubble is for an intelligent investor to return to more organized and scientific methods of industry and stock valuation and always to avoid investing in any asset price bubbles in any industry, however tempting this might look short-term.

# CHAPTER 24

# SUMMARY OF US FINANCIAL CRISES &
# THE RESILIENCE OF THE AMERICAN SPIRIT:
# LESSONS TO BE LEARNED

Basic Ingredients of the U.S. Economy

The first ingredient of a nation's economic system is its natural resources. The United States is rich in mineral resources and fertile farm soil, and it is blessed with a moderate climate. It also has extensive coastlines on both the Atlantic and Pacific Oceans, as well as on the Gulf of Mexico. Rivers flow from far within the continent, and the Great Lakes -- five large, inland lakes along the U.S. border with Canada -- provide additional shipping access. These extensive waterways have helped shape the country's economic growth over the years and helped bind America's 50 individual states together in a single economic unit.

The second ingredient is labor, which converts natural resources into goods. The number of available workers and, more importantly, their productivity help determine the health of an economy. Throughout its history, the United States has experienced steady growth in the labor force, and that, in turn, has helped fuel almost constant economic expansion.

Until shortly after World War I, most workers were immigrants from Europe, their immediate descendants, or African-Americans whose ancestors were brought to the Americas as slaves. In the early years of the 20th century, large numbers of Asians immigrated to the United States, while many Latin American immigrants came in later years Although the United States has experienced some periods of high unemployment and other times when labor was in short supply, immigrants tended to come when jobs were plentiful. Often willing to work for somewhat lower wages than acculturated workers, they generally prospered, earning far more than they would have in their native lands. The nation prospered as well, so that the economy grew fast enough to absorb even more newcomers

The quality of available labor -- how hard people are willing to work and how skilled they are -- is at least as important to a country's economic success as the number of workers. In the early days of the United States, frontier life required hard work, and what is known as the Protestant work ethic reinforced that trait. A strong emphasis on education, including technical and vocational training, also contributed to America's economic success, as did a willingness to experiment and to change.

Labor mobility has likewise been important to the capacity of the American economy to adapt to changing conditions. When immigrants flooded labor markets on the East Coast, many workers moved inland, often to farmland waiting to be tilled. Similarly, economic opportunities in industrial, northern cities attracted black Americans from southern farms in the first half of the 20th century.

Labor-force quality continues to be an important issue. Today, Americans consider "human capital" a key to success in numerous modern, high-technology industries. As a result, government leaders and business officials increasingly stress the importance of education and training to develop workers with the kind of nimble minds and adaptable skills needed in new industries such as computers and telecommunications.

But natural resources and labor account for only part of an economic system. These resources must be organized and directed as efficiently as possible. In the American economy, managers, responding to signals from markets, perform this function. The traditional managerial structure in America is based on a top-down chain of command; authority flows from the chief executive in the boardroom, who makes sure that the entire business runs smoothly and efficiently, through various lower levels of management responsible for coordinating different parts of the enterprise, down to the foreman on the shop floor. Numerous tasks are divided among different divisions and workers.

In early 20th-century America, this specialization, or division of labor, was said to reflect "scientific management" based on systematic analysis.

Many enterprises continue to operate with this traditional structure, but others have taken changing views on management. Facing heightened global competition, American businesses are seeking more flexible organization structures, especially in high-technology industries that employ skilled workers and must develop, modify, and even customize products rapidly. Excessive hierarchy and division of labor increasingly are thought to inhibit creativity. As a result, many companies have "flattened" their organizational structures, reduced the number of managers, and delegated more authority to interdisciplinary teams of workers

In every economic system, entrepreneurs and managers bring together natural resources, labor, and technology to produce and distribute goods and services. But the way these different elements are organized and used also reflects a nation's political ideals and its culture.

The United States is often described as a "capitalist" economy, a term coined by 19th-century German economist and social theorist Karl Marx to describe a system in which a small group of people who control large amounts of money, or capital, make the most important economic decisions. Marx contrasted capitalist economies to "socialist" ones, which vest more power in the political system. Marx and his followers believed that capitalist economies concentrate power in the hands of wealthy business people, who aim mainly to maximize profits; socialist economies, on the other hand, would be more likely to feature greater control by government, which tends to put political aims -- a more equal distribution of society's resources, for instance -- ahead of profits.

While those categories, though oversimplified, have elements of truth to them, they are far less relevant today. If the pure capitalism described by Marx ever existed, it has long since disappeared, as governments in the United States and many other countries have intervened in their economies to limit concentrations of power and address many of the social problems associated with unchecked private commercial interests. As a result, the American economy is perhaps better described as a "mixed" economy, with government playing an important role along with private enterprise.

Although Americans often disagree about exactly where to draw the line between their beliefs in free enterprise and government management, the mixed economy they have developed has been remarkably successful.

*This chapter is dedicated to the US Department of State for its contribution to about.com*

# CHAPTER 25

## WHY THE AMERICAN WAY OF LIFE WILL PERSIST AND SUCCEED

Since the birth of a new country in the eighteenth century, the United States has always persisted. This has been in no small measure to the great and marvelous courage of both its citizens and the new immigrants who arrived here from far away shores. If you study the financial history of the United States over two centuries, you will note that there has been one financial catastrophe after other. Although such catastrophes have spelt havoc in the short-run and loss of fortunes and jobs, the economy has always jumped back to its feet.

America has always had to grapple with challenges and disadvantages. This started out when our forefathers came from Europe to establish a better life for themselves. Escaping the caste system and social discrimination prevalent in countries like the United Kingdom, Americans new and old have had a starry eye and a long term dream: the dream of liberty, life and the pursuit of Happiness. In the presence of great adversity and uncertainty they have managed to come on top of some very difficult personal and business conditions. I have travelled all over this beautiful Planet but nowhere and I mean nowhere have I seen a more courageous, enterprising individual as an American.

This economic and materialistic survival has been aided by the philosophy and ideas of Adam Smith, who promoted a laissez faire attitude, recommending government stay out of individual and corporate matters.

Free trade, the right to individual liberty, a level playing field and a justice system to enforce equality in rights have all helped expand and strengthen the American economy. Americans must be truly proud of their heritage, their free enterprise system and a solid well organized financial network.

One must not forget the great contributions of Alexander Hamilton, who in a period of few years revolutionized the entire US financial system. Immigrants entering the nation with unlimited talents and genius combined with an environment supporting excellence in the arts, sciences and humanities have made America a great super-power.

America will persist and succeed economically. However, it is important for Americans to understand their financial rights and accept the impending challenge to maneuver their investments to maximize their wealth; this responsibility lies in individual hands. The great financial and credit crisis, which started in the Fall of 2007 has taught Americans to be more careful with their finances. Spend less, save more, get rid of unnecessary credit and focus on the simple and significant parts of Life (like your family and children and philanthropy) are the new Mantra.

Every American faces an individual challenge today to stay away from the fraudsters and con artists and fashion their investments in a way where they have enough to live well today and in the future. To this thought and goal is the three book series entitled, "Quantum Crisis," dedicated.

# CHAPTER 26

## CONCLUSION

This narrative provides a 360 degree view of all critical financial crises in the last four hundred years. You are now ready to read "Quantum Crisis II—The Great Financial and Credit Crisis of 2007–2009." This book will provide you with the facts, figures and manifestations of the current global financial and credit crisis. Once you have completed reading this book, I would urge you to read "Quantum Crisis III". This book  entitled, "Quantum Crisis III–Winning Investment Strategies to Prosper through the 2007–2009 Global Financial and Credit Crisis," will show an average investor how to save, grow and protect one's financial nest–egg. I hope you have enjoyed this historical narrative. Happy and Successful Financial Sailing to all of you.

Best wishes for your continued financial success!!!!!!!!!!

# CONSULTATIVE APPENDIX

# QUANTUM CRISIS II-
## THE GREAT FINANCIAL AND CREDIT CRISIS
## 2007-2009

# TABLE OF CONTENTS

# PART 2 - THE REAL FINANCIAL & CREDIT CRISIS 2007-2009

CHAPTER 5

**BACKGROUND OF PAST GLOBAL FINANCIAL CRISES**

TYPES OF FINANCIAL CRISES

BANKING CRISES

SPECULATIVE BUBBLES AND CRASHES

INTERNATIONAL FINANCIAL CRISES

WIDER ECONOMIC CRISES

CAUSES AND CONSEQUENCES OF FINANCIAL CRISES

LEVERAGE

ASSET-LIABILITY MISMATCH

UNCERTAINTY AND HERD BEHAVIOR

REGULATORY FAILURES

FRAUD

CONTAGION

RECESSIONARY EFFECTS

THEORIES OF FINANCIAL CRISES

WORLD SYSTEMS THEORY

MINSKY'S THEORY

CO-ORDINATION GAMES

HERDING MODELS AND LEARNING MODELS

CHAPTER 6

**TIMELINE OF GLOBAL FINANCIAL CRISIS OF 2007-2009**

PRE-PANIC PHASE

PRELUDE TO PANIC PHASE

START OF THE FINANCIAL CRISIS

CHAPTER 11

**THE LEHMAN BROTHERS FIASCO**
BACKGROUND
CAUSES OF BANKRUPTCY
EFFECTS OF LEHMAN BANKRUPTCY
MORAL OF THE STORY

CHAPTER 12

**CONTROVERSY BEHIND FREDDIE MAC AND FANNIE MAE**
ORIGINS
ACCOUNTING ERRORS
GSE'S & THE GLOBAL FINANCIAL AND CREDIT CRISIS
MORAL OF THE STORY

CHAPTER 13

**THE COLLAPSE OF WASHINGTON MUTUAL**
BACKGROUND
HISTORY
ENTER THE SUB-PRIME MESS
EFFECTS OF CLOSURE
MORAL OF THE STORY
CHAPTER 14

**THE DEMISE OF THE INVESTMENT BANKING INDUSTRY
AND WALL STREET**
TARP (TROUBLED ASSET RELIEF PROGRAM) RECIPIENTS
USE OF TARP MONEY
MORGAN STANLEY AND THE GLOBAL CRISIS
GOLDMAN SACHS AND THE GLOBAL CRISIS
MORAL OF THE STORY

CHAPTER 15
**THE CITIGROUP FIASCO**
BACKGROUND
HISTORY
CITIBANK AND THE SUB-PRIME MORTGAGE CRISIS
CITIBANK GOES OUT WITH THE BEGGAR BOWL
CITIBANK AND THE SHADOW BANKING SYSTEM
CITIBANK AND THE US GOVT. BAILOUT PLAN
MARKET REACTION TO CITI FINANCIAL POSITION
NATIONALIZATION OF CITI
IMPLICATION FOR CITI SHAREHOLDERS AND BOND
HOLDERS
INSIDE SPECULATION BY CITI SENIOR MANAGEMENT
MORAL OF THE STORY

CHAPTER 16

**FINANCIAL PROBLEMS AT BANK OF AMERICA**
THE GOVT.BROKERED PURCHASE OF COUNTRYWIDE GROUP
THE GOVT. SPONSORED PURCHASE OF MERRILL LYNCH
THE FIRING OF THAIN'S
CONTINUAL WEAKNESS IN ASSET QUALITY AND HIGH
LEVERAGE IN MBS'S
BANK OF AMERICA-- SHARE PRICE DECIMATION
BANK OF AMERICA: A RECIPIENT OF TARP FUNDS
BACKSTOPPING OF BAD LOANS AT MERRILL AMONG
OTHERS
TALKS OF NATIONALIZATION AND POTENTIAL
IMPLICATIONS TO SHAREHOLDERS

CHAPTER 25
**BANKRUPTCY OF ICELAND**
BACKGROUND
HISTORY
THE BANKING CRISIS
CAUSES OF BANKING CRISIS
LESSONS TO BE LEARNT FROM CRISIS
TIMELINE OF FINANCIAL CRISIS
MORAL OF STORY
CHAPTER 26
**THE IMPACT OF FINANCIAL& CREDIT CRISIS ON AUSTRALASIA**
THE INDIA SITUATION
INDIAN BANKING
NEGATIVE FALLOUT FROM CRISIS
CHINA AND THE GLOBAL CRISIS
FALLOUT FROM THE FINANCIAL AND CREDIT CRISIS
THE JAPANESE SCENARIO
JAPANESE ISSUES
HISTORY OF CRISIS
OVERALL EFFECT OF THE CRISIS
THE AUSTRALIAN SITUATION

CHAPTER 27
**THE MADOFF PONZI SCANDAL IN THE UNITED STATES**
BACKGROUND
CURRENT DEVELOPMENTS
BIGGER ISSUES

CHAPTER 29 (CONTINUED)

MARKET VOLATILITY WITHIN 401(k) AND US RETIREMENT PLANS

FEDERAL RESERVE OF THE US LOWERS INTEREST RATES

LEGISLATION

FEDERAL RESERVE RESPONSE

EUROPEAN UNION RESPONSE

POLITICAL EFFECTS AND PROJECTIONS RELATED TO THE ECONOMIC CRISIS

A SPECIAL NOTE ON US GOVERNMENT INITIATIVES

THE EMERGENCY ECONOMIC STABILIZATION ACT OF 2008

INITIATIVES BY THE OBAMA ADMINISTRATION

NEW STIMULUS PLAN

DETAILS OF NEW STIMULUS PLAN

MAKING WORK PAY CREDIT

CHILD TAX CREDIT

AMERICAN OPPORTUNITY TAX CREDIT

ALTERNATIVE MINIMUM TAX (AMT)

OTHER PROVISIONS

THE AMERICAN RECOVERY AND REINVESTMENT ACT, 2009

COMPARISON OF HOUSE, SENATE & CONFERENCE VERSIONS

CONFERENCE REPORT

PROVISIONS OF THE ACT

CONCLUSION

# PART 3: WHAT WENT WRONG AND HOW TO FIX THE PROBLEM PERMANENTLY

CHAPTER 30
**THE WORLD FINANCIAL SYSTEM EXPLAINED**
BACKGROUND
FINANCIAL ARCHITECTURE
INTERNATIONAL INSTITUTIONS WHICH CONTROL THE GFS
GOVT. INSTITUTIONS WHO PLAY A ROLE IN THE GFS
PRIVATE PLAYERS IN THE GLOBAL FINANCIAL SYSTEM (GFS)
THE WASHINGTON CONSENSUS
WORLD TRADE v GLOBAL FINANCIAL SERVICES
THE FINANCIAL STABILITY FORUM

CHAPTER 31
**COMPREHENSIVE UNDERSTANDING OF THE GLOBAL FINANCIAL CRISIS**
BACKGROUND
TRANSFORMATION OF PROBLEM TO BANKING CRISIS
TRANSFORMATION OF BANKING CRISIS TO STOCK MARKET CRASH & CREDIT CRISIS
TRANFORMATION TO REAL ECONOMY DAMAGE
GLOBALIZATION OF FINANCIAL MARKETS
ISSUES

CHAPTER 32
## COMPREHENSIVE UNDERSTANDING OF THE GLOBAL CREDIT CRISIS
MARKET SIZE AND PARTICIPANTS
KEY UNFUNDED CREDIT DERIVATIVE PRODUCTS
CREDIT DEFAULT SWAP
TOTAL RETURN SWAP
KEY FUNDED CREDIT DERIVATIVE PRODUCTS
COLLATERIZED DEBT OBLIGATIONS
CREDIT DERIVATIVES AND THE GLOBAL BANKING CRISIS

CHAPTER 33
## THE ROLE & RESPONSIBILITY OF THE FEDERAL RESERVE & FANNIE MAE/FREDDIE MAC IN AMPLIFYING THE CRISIS
BACKGROUND
THE CREATION OF FANNIE MAE AND FREDDIE MAC
THE ROLE OF FEDERAL RESERVE IN AMPLIFYING THE CRISIS

CHAPTER 34
## INDICATORS OF THE BROAD CRISIS
THE ONGOING US HEALTH AND MEDICARE CRISIS
THE PROBLEM
THE SOLUTION
THE GLOBAL WARMING CRISIS
THE PROBLEM
THE SOLUTION
US DEPENDENCE ON FOREIGN OIL
THE NOTORIOUS OVERSPENDING BY US GOVT. AND AMERICANS

# CONSULTATIVE APPENDIX

## QUANTUM CRISIS III-
WINNING INVESTMENT STRATEGIES TO PROSPER THROUGH THE
2007-09 GLOBAL FINANCIAL AND CREDIT CRISIS

# TABLE OF CONTENTS

# SECTION 1
# FUNDAMENTAL FINANCIAL PLANNING CONCEPTS

CHAPTER 5
*THE FIRST PILLAR OF YOUR FINANCIAL FOUNDATION:*
*SAVINGS*
LEARN TO SAVE FIRST
THE PIGGY BANK EPISODE
THE CANADIAN BANK BOOK EPISODE
THE AMERICAN SAVINGS QUANDARY

CHAPTER 6
*THE SECOND PILLAR OF YOUR FINANCIAL FOUNDATION:*
*INVESTMENTS*
LEARN TO INVEST--- SIMPLE LESSONS IN INVESTING
MASLOW'S MODEL OF HUMAN NEEDS
RAJPAL INVESTMENT SUITABILITY PYRAMID

CHAPTER 7
*THE THIRD PILLAR OF YOUR FINANCIAL FOUNDATION:*
*RISK MANAGEMENT*
LEARN TO PROTECT:
YOUR LOVED ONES
YOUR BUSINESS
YOUR RETIREMENT INCOME NEEDS
YOUR CHILDREN'S EDUCATION NEEDS
YOUR WEALTH IN EVENT OF DISABILITY

CHAPTER 12
*PUTTING YOUR INVESTMENT PLAN TOGETHER*
DETAILED EXPLANATION & ANALYSIS OF PERSONAL
INVESTMENT PLANNING
PORTFOLIO COMPENSATION & RISK DIVERSIFICATION


CHAPTER 13
*PLANNING & PROTECTING AGAINST FUTURE THREATS
TO YOUR FINANCIAL SECURITY*
THREAT OF MARRIAGE BREAKDOWN—PRE/POST NUPTIAL
AGREEMENT
THREAT OF BUSINESS PARTNER CONFLICT------
CHALLENGE OF PROPERLY DRAFTED PARTNERSHIP
AGREEMENT
THREAT OF ALL OTHER POTENTIAL LITIGATION---
LIABILITY COVERAGE REQUIREMENTS
BANKRUPTCY THREAT—SETTING EFFECTIVE FINANCIAL
AND LEGAL STRUCTURES PRIOR TO BANKRUPTCY

# SECTION 2
## ADVANCED INVESTMENT TECHNIQUES


CHAPTER 14
**OVERALL RISK MANAGEMENT STRATEGY FOR THE
ORDINARY INVESTOR**
WHAT IS RISK MANAGEMENT
UNDERSTANDING OF LIFE, DISABILITY,
GROUP AND HEALTH INSURANCE

CHAPTER 15
INVESTMENT/ASSET ALLOCATION STRATEGIES
FOR THE SMART INVESTOR

CHAPTER 16
SUPERCHARGING YOUR RETIREMENT STRATEGY
CHAPTER 17
COLLEGE FUNDING STRATEGIES

CHAPTER 18
HOUSE MORTGAGE, HOUSE REFINANCING &
HOME INVESTMENT STRATEGIES

CHAPTER 19
CREDIT CARD DEBT REDUCTION STRATEGIES

CHAPTER 20
COMPREHENSIVE INSURANCE STRATEGIES
WITH PRIORITIZATION OBJECTIVES

CHAPTER 21
SAVINGS STRATEGIES FOR WEALTH GENERATION

CHAPTER 22
SMALL BUSINESS WEALTH CREATION STRATEGIES

# SECTION 3
# PERSONAL GROWTH STRATEGIES FOR WEALTH ACCELERATION

CHAPTER 23
*SELF-DEVELOPMENT STRATEGIES*
THE ROLE OF GOAL SETTING AND MOTIVATION
GOAL MONITORING AND EVALUATION

CHAPTER 24
PERSONAL HEALTH AND WELLBEING STRATEGIES

CHAPTER 25
SPIRITUAL STRATEGIES FOR A HAPPIER AND BALANCED LIFE

CHAPTER 26
PERSONAL RELATIONSHIP STRATEGIES FOR A
CONFLICT-FREE LIFE IN TOUGH TIMES

CHAPTER 27
SUMMARY

CHAPTER 28
CONCLUSION

## SUMMARY OF ILLUSTRATIONS

ILLUSTRATION 1
PIGGY BANK

ILLUSTRATION 2
MASLOW'S MODEL –HIERARCHY OF HUMAN NEEDS

ILLUSTRATION 3
RAJPAL INVESTMENT SUITABILITY PYRAMID©

ILLUSTRATION 4A
INVESTOR– INSURANCE COMPANY RELATIONSHIP

ILLUSTRATION 4B
LIST OF INVESTOR CONTINGENCIES

ILLUSTRATION 4C
LIST OF CONTINGENCIES (CONTINUED)

ILLUSTRATION 5
SAMPLE BUY–SELL PARTNERSHIP AGREEMENT
FUNDED BY LIFE INSURANCE

ILLUSTRATION 6
TAX FREE VS TAXABLE INVESTMENT

ILLUSTRATION 7A
NET SURPLUS INCOME COUNTS

ILLUSTRATION 7B
THE FASTEST WAY TO GET RICH

ILLUSTRATION 8
PUTTING ALL THE PIECES OF YOUR
YOUR FINANCIAL PLAN TOGETHER

ILLUSTRATION 9
SIMPLIFIED EXPOSITION OF FINANCIAL PLANNING

ILLUSTRATION 10
 INVESTMENT POSSIBILITIES: RISK –RETURN SCENARIOS

ILLUSTRATION 11
DIFFERENT MODEL PORTFOLIOS

### "QUANTUM CRISIS II
### - The Great Financial and Credit Crisis 2007-2009"
### ($ 29 USD-Free shipping)

The second installment of the 3-book series entitled, "Quantum Crisis." This book starts its exposition with the beginnings of the global financial crisis, commencing in the Fall of 2007. It proceeds beautifully to sequentially elaborate on all significant developments of this crisis. A special section deals with retaliatory steps taken by world governments to stem the crisis: it ends with the author's set of recommendations in terms of how to overcome this crisis effectively. This book is a great read for anyone interested in:

(a)   Understanding the current financial and credit crisis and

(b) Comprehending the investor challenge to save, grow and protect one's wealth in turbulent times.

## "QUANTUM CRISIS III
### Winning Investment Strategies to Prosper through the Global Financial and Credit Crisis"
### ($39 USD-Free shipping)

This publication marks the final installment of the 3 book series entitled Quantum Crisis. This book deals with specific investment strategies to assist an investor save, grow and protect his hard earned wealth. It starts with a section on Basic Financial Planning concepts and then graduates to discussion of advanced investment strategies. It concludes with an understanding of health and other wellbeing strategies, suggesting that a total balance of physical, emotional, mental and spiritual factors assist in building not only a financially successful Life but also a happy one. A great read for any individual wanting to learn to employ better investment and insurance techniques to grow his wealth in Challenging financial times.

## "OFFSHORE INVESTMENTS
### -The Millionaire Vision."
### $99 USD(Free Shipping)

This book deals with the challenges of investing in offshore locations. It explains brilliantly the basic investment principles involved in saving, growing and protecting your capital. Then it deals with the advantages and drawbacks of world offshore centers. It continues with an understanding of trusts, foundations and other asset protection mechanisms. A must read for anyone planning to diversify his investment portfolio offshore!!!!!

## "OFFSHORE HAVENS
### -"The four best kept secrets of millionaires."
### $99 USD(Free Shipping)

This book presents the top four offshore havens in the world in terms of the most important factors of superiority: privacy, safety, wealth management services and availability of professional expertise. The book then proceeds to explain the advantages/drawbacks of each of these top four centers. In the process it deals with current tax and investment legislation for international investments. This is a great book for international investors who seek advanced tax, investment and asset protection knowledge.

## "YOU HAVE IT ALL-
## Your Life is yours to truly discover and enjoy."
## $29 USD(Free Shipping)

The author takes you through a marvelous journey, which ultimately questions the value of money in its relationship to Personal Happiness. Through his real Life experiences with his clients, the author discovered that Successful Living challenges one to achieve an optimal balance between Material pursuits and Happiness. He suggests means, methods and processes to live a more balanced and integrated Life leading to Wealth and Happiness simultaneously. A valuable book for anyone aspiring to Wealth and Happiness!!!!!

## "QUANTUM SELLING"
## $ 29 USD(Free Shipping)

This book deals with modern, practical and time-tested methods of achieving success in any Sales Endeavor. Through his business and sales experience of more than twenty years, culminating in achievement of all the top business awards in North America, the writer expounds a simple, time -proven technology of finding, growing and retaining clients in any field of business. This book is a must read for anyone desirous of building a successful Sales Practice/New business.

## "QUANTUM SALES MANAGEMENT"
## $ 29 USD(Free Shipping)

This publication focuses on proven success methods essential to the optimal management of a sales force. It discusses brilliant ideas addressing the four major challenges in professional sales management----- recruiting, training, developing and motivating salespeople. The research in this book is based on live studies and experiences of the author, who captured every major management award in North America, both at the corporate and professional body level in his field of financial service management. This book is extremely valuable to both new and experienced sales managers, who want to increase their sales numbers and achieve an even higher level of professional success.

## "QUANTUM MARKETING"
## How to create & grow profitable business opportunities
## $ 29 USD(Free shipping)

This publication deals with the time-honored principles of marketing management. This book is truly unique in the sense that it approaches marketing from a 360 degree view. It does this by focusing on all aspects of marketing management, starting from the traditional 4 P's (Product, Price, Promotion and Place) to more elaborate concepts of the psychological, societal and philosophical implications of the marketing process. A must read for both marketing practitioners and enlightened marketing students, who want a deeper and significant understanding of the marketing process and their role in it.

## "QUANTUM ETHICS"
## $29 USD(Free shipping)

This book deals with some of the ethical concerns besetting the world today. It specifically discusses how major world corporations have ripped customers, investors and government authorities in their blind pursuit of money and fame. It throws a fresh light on some of the major world scandals and proposes ways and means of organizing, controlling and delivering a higher quality of ethical care to consumers. Through the process, it provides an understanding of the twin challenges of World Sustainability and Global Warming------these constitute two of the most important ethical considerations of our age. A great book for anyone interested in exploring how Ethics and Business clash and how to protect oneself from dishonesty, misrepresentation and poor business practice.

## "QUANTUM PUBLIC SPEAKING"
## How to Influence People through Superlative Communication(29 USD-Free Shipping)

Here, for once, is a fresh and entertaining book on Effective Public Speaking. The author has shared his twenty plus years of experience as a major public speaker, debater and trainer of sales people. This brilliant and enjoyable book discusses how anyone can master Public Speaking through one-on-one communication and in group public speaking. A must read for anyone who wants to increase his communication power with a view to positively influencing people!!!!!

**BOOKS CAN BE ORDERED DIRECTLY AT:**
**www.pioneer-communication.com or at**
**rdrajpal@yahoo.com**

10% DISCOUNT FOR 2-3 BOOKS
15% DISCOUNT FOR 4-5 BOOKS
20% DISCOUNT FOR 6-7 BOOKS
25% DISCOUNT FOR MORE THAN 7 BOOKS

**** NOTE ALL BOOKS MUST BE ORDERED AT
THE SAME TIME FOR DISCOUNT TO APPLY
FREE SHIPPING AND DISCOUNTS ONLY PROVIDED WHEN
ORDERS PLACED DIRECTLY AT ABOVE WEBSITE
FREE SHIPPING APPLIES ONLY TO CONTINENTAL
UNITED STATES DELIVERY